Search Your Self

365 Meditations
for the Mind, Body,
and Soul

Scott M. Gallagher

Eagle Brook

William Morrow and Company, Inc.

New York

Copyright © 2000 by Scott M. Gallagher

Published by Eagle Brook
An Imprint of William Morrow and Company, Inc.
1350 Avenue of the Americas, New York, N.Y. 10019

It is the policy of William Morrow and Company, Inc.,
and its imprints and affiliates, recognizing the importance of preserving what has been written, to print
the books we publish on acid-free paper, and we
exert our best efforts to that end.

Library of Congress Cataloging-in-Publication Data

Gallagher, Scott M.
Search your self : 365 meditations for the mind,
body, and soul / Scott M. Gallagher.—1st ed.
            p   cm.
ISBN 0-688-17093-5 (alk. paper)
1. Conduct of life. I. Title.
BJ1581.2.G35   2000
158.1'28—dc21   99-041550

Printed in the United States of America

First Edition

1 2 3 4 5 6 7 8 9 10

BOOK DESIGN BY JENNIFER ANN DADDIO

www.williammorrow.com

For my son, Dylan

Acknowledgments

A loving and heartfelt thank-you goes to my mother, Patricia Niesenbaum, for instilling in me the love of great literature; and to my father, Jack Gallagher, for providing me the wherewithal to pursue such a precarious vocation as writing.

I wish to acknowledge my brothers, John, David, and Marc, as well as Dr. Leonard Niesenbaum and Kim Gallagher.

All the people past and present at Alchemy Communications, Inc., the creators of The Mind, Body & Soul Network (www.mindbodysoul.com), without whom this book wouldn't have been possible: Christine, Jennifer, Rob, Justin, Bruce, Kevin, Melina, Elaine, and most especially Eric Lowe and Nolan Quan.

Thanks and appreciation go to Diana De Bartlo for passing along my proposal for this book to Michelle Shinseki, my insightful and wonderful editor at Eagle Brook.

Finally, I need to express my gratitude to my friends Greg Cuneo, Robert "the Great" Santini, Wayne Hubler, Wayne Hagendorf, and Jerry Stewart.

Introduction

I feel compelled to confess at the outset that in this book I'm practicing spirituality without a license. Alas, I'm not a particle physicist gone mystic, nor a new-age psychiatrist. I don't know the twelve laws of instant enlightenment or the ten steps to happiness and success. I haven't been to India for a name change or to a Buddhist monastery in Japan for an orange robe—I haven't even been to India or Japan. I'm not a guru, philosopher, minister, medicine man, or even an astrologer but just a regular guy, an average person not unlike yourself, who through a happy concurrence of circumstances found himself writing the "Daily Meditations" column for The Mind, Body & Soul Network (www.mindbodysoul.com), the Internet's largest self-help site.

Little did I know when I accepted this assignment in April 1998 what a deeply moving and eye-opening experience it would become. The job itself seemed quite simple—not to mention exciting and fun, as I fancied myself a writer—find some inspiring quotations and then comment on them. "Sure thing," I said, and then set to work.

Well, over a year later, after searching through thousands of quotations and spending countless hours meditating on and writing about the quotations I chose, I can tell you I'm not the same person I was when I began this . . . this what? . . . this labor of love. To be sure, the contemplation required to adequately comment on quotes by such eminent people as Emerson, Lao-tzu, Einstein, Wilde, Goethe, Cicero, and Mother Teresa can't help but effect an internal revolution.

Which brings us to this book: a collection of 365 quotations with comments, one for each day of the year. As for the quotations themselves, I tried to pick only those authors with whose work I was familiar and whose particular quotations I found profoundly engaging. Thus you will find in these pages that certain authors appear more than once (for example, Buddha and Thoreau). Nevertheless, I did my best to choose a diverse group from which to quote: philosophers, poets, novelists, scientists, religious figures from various religions, and proverbs from various countries.

Now, concerning the comments, or meditations, if you find in them more affection than brilliance, more feeling than formula, more heart than head, and more question than answer, that's my inclination. My intention was never to say "Today you should take several deep breaths and forget your worries" or "Today you should spend the day pampering yourself." To inspire your mind and inform your senses, to make you rethink what you've thought and to question what you've taken for granted as I had to do when responding to these quotations, is the spirit in which I wrote these meditations, and to the extent to which you are provoked to think is the extent to which I've accomplished my task. Search Your Self.

*It is a good thing to read books of
quotations, the quotations when engraved on the memory
give you good thoughts.*
—Winston Churchill

*The wisdom of the wise and the experience of the ages
are perpetuated by quotations.*
—Benjamin Disraeli

*The teachings of elegant sayings
Should be collected when one can.
For the supreme gift of words of wisdom,
Any price will be paid.*
—Nāgārjuna

*All truly wise thoughts have been thought already thousands
of times, but to make them truly ours, we must think them over again
honestly, till they take root in our personal experience.*
—Johann Wolfgang von Goethe

Search Your Self

DAY 1 ✦ Teaching

*To live a single day and hear a good teaching is better than
to live a hundred years without knowing such teaching.*
—Buddha

Good teaching is more available than we might be aware of. We
spend countless days unaware of the lessons that everywhere
abound. That person you dislike and constantly argue with, he or
she is your teacher. That shy person you ignore, he or she is
your teacher. That special person you love, he or she is your
teacher. The children you see at play, they are your teachers.
Yes, good teaching comes in many guises. For instance, a tree
can teach us many things, and so can the sun, moon, sea, and
stars. Life abounds in good teachings; it just needs more willing
students.

Activate yourself to duty by remembering your position, who
you are, and what you have obliged yourself to be.
—*Thomas à Kempis*

All too often we find ourselves traveling down a road that we'd rather not be on. Somewhere along the way we've gotten away from our purpose. Somehow we've gotten sidetracked.

This may last a month or many years, though it's not the duration, but the realization, that matters. To awaken and get back on track—this is the important thing. To ease back into our appointed purpose—this has meaning.

Misdirected, we know a restlessness in our gut. Misguided, we know an uncertainty in our days.

It takes tremendous courage for us to admit to ourselves that we've been traveling on the detour road for far too long. Many choose to look the other way rather than make such a confession. Yet the only way for us to get back on the proper route is to have the presence of mind to acknowledge that we're lost.

DAY 3 ◆ State of Mind

Why should we think upon things that are lovely?
Because thinking determines life. It is a common habit to blame life
upon the environment. Environment modifies life but does not govern life.
The soul is stronger than its surroundings.
—William James

Too much negative thinking and we foul our own environment. Through negativity the nimbus that surrounds us grows pale, and though we walk on polished floors, life becomes colorless.

Should your surroundings be bringing you down, paint the walls—and then change your thinking. Ugliness cannot be denied, nor should it be ignored, but neither should it be dwelt upon and thereby made into the cause and excuse for unhappiness.

What portion of clarity and beauty we behold and possess begins with the quality of our thinking, the context and shape of our perspective.

The environment modifies, but it is the soul that rules and purifies a life. See to it, therefore, that you heed the state of your soul more than you do the state of your residence.

DAY 4 ✦ Wonder

Wisdom begins in wonder.
—*Socrates*

Consider a caterpillar . . . its metamorphosis from the ugly to the beautiful. Look now as if flits about from flower to flower on its impressionistic wings! Is not its honeyed journey amazing, wonderful, a joy to behold?

Consider the child . . . its seemingly inexhaustible capacity for wonder. Look how interested, how deeply involved it gets with the most commonplace objects—shoes, boxes, keys, furniture—anything and everything within reach of its soft, grasping hands needs to be touched (and, if possible, tasted).

Surely, for any adult alive, the wonderment of the child in itself is a source of wonder. Perhaps, the child is here for just this purpose, to awaken us, to show us again how to wonder, how to be awed by the familiar.

Life requires that we relearn this fresh vision, and again see with the eyes of a child, lest our lives become a hopeless routine, a terrible bore. Seeing daily life's startling diversity, this is our duty as mindful human beings.

Consider the mountains. . . . Consider the clouds. . . . Consider the sunset. . . .

DAY 5 ✦ Fixing Faults

The greatest of all faults, I should say,
is to be conscious of none.
—Thomas Carlyle

Undoubtedly, we first need to be self-aware enough to acknowledge our faults before we can do anything in terms of finding a solution.

However, to be conscious of our own shortcomings is one thing, but to do something about them is quite another. Many of us are aware of our fears, insecurities, and limitations. Yet, instead of searching for a solution, we excuse them by saying, "Well, that's just the way I am."

But are we sure it has to be this way? Are we certain that an insecurity is an insecurity is an insecurity and a fear is a fear is a fear? Or have our fears and insecurities been with us so long that we've never even considered questioning them?

Who knows but that with a little patience and effort we may yet succeed in uprooting some of these long-lived limitations.

*Have courage for the great sorrows of life and
patience for the small ones.*
—*Victor Hugo*

Look at the Humpty Dumpty–type lives we lead. We have such a tenuous hold that any hard-luck event may shatter us. And, as you well know, the tragic possibilities are endless. Indeed, the older we get, the closer to the edge we sit, until finally we are precariously perched on the brink of our own demise.

Alas, what's to be done? Certainly we shouldn't dwell on such things, as that would make us too morose and sullen. Maybe we should just see sorrow as sorrow and know that it feels as it does, like sorrow, and that it's part and parcel of being human and alive, and that it has its place.

Otherwise, the losses we inevitably suffer as we traverse our way into old age leave us in pieces—and, you know the rest . . . "All the king's horses and all the king's men . . ."

It is the mark of an educated mind to be able to entertain
a thought without accepting it.
—Aristotle

When someone says of you that you have an "open mind," surely this must be what that person means. An open mind implies an informed mind—and not necessarily a formally educated mind—a mind capable of listening without being easily persuaded, a mind capable of thinking without immediately concluding, a mind capable of separating wheat from chaff. Any one of us who's met an unschooled person blessed with common sense, what we sometimes call "horse sense," who may not be able to quote Aristotle or has not even heard of him, but surely knows which way the wind blows, can attest to this.

Solitude, though it may be silent as light, is like light,
the mightiest of agencies; for solitude is essential to man. All men
come into this world alone; all leave it alone.
—*Thomas De Quincey*

I know some people who will never be alone yet will always be lonely. They are in and out of relationships, surrounded by friends and family, yet nothing can quench their unslakable thirst for loneliness. To be sure, this is why they can't maintain a relationship, though they are always in one. Constantly searching outwardly for someone to fill their cup, they quickly and inevitably grow dissatisfied and seek fulfillment at another well when the current one dries—as it always does for them. Tragic, really, this restlessness of spirit.

Meanwhile the stories of betrayal, heartbreak, and loss grow legion. So what gives then? Married or not, are we all simply fated to the disquiet of loneliness? Perhaps if we step back from these manic attempts at self-satisfaction in the arms of another, this clinging that we engage in, we can begin to see the possibility of being alone—or with someone—without feeling lonely.

DAY 9 ✦ Self-Knowledge

To know oneself is enlightenment.
Tao Te Ching

This idea courses through history like the Nile River. On the oracle at Delphi in ancient Greece, the saying "Know Thyself" was inscribed. Shakespeare wrote "to thine own self be true . . ." We must consider, therefore, understanding ourselves to be of the utmost importance. Not only because so many eminent people have said so, but also because, as any intelligent person can see, it is of the first importance.

By understanding ourselves—how we think, how we react, how we feel—we then begin to understand and appreciate this dynamic, inhabited world. Understanding ourselves is the first and last step to feeling at home within and without. The entire beauty of a life depends on this ongoing process of understanding.

A lioness, a yellow rose, a pink salmon, a red-tailed hawk, a jellyfish, an oak tree, a single-cell anemone, all are in complete agreement with themselves and so with the world. Their beauty is self-evident; often, ours is not.

Let us then take the time to cultivate an understanding of ourselves and so begin blooming from within, flowering colorfully into the awaiting world.

People that seem so glorious are all show;
underneath they are like everyone else.
—Euripides

Take away the new car, the fancy clothes, the dark sunglasses, and all the other finery and what's left? Just the wind and your character, and no amount of personal pomp and circumstance can disguise a deeply flawed character.

You may look polished and slick in your tuxedo but the expression you wear is sad and lonely. Your sequined gown may turn heads but your walk is anxious and uncertain.

What may be glorious in our appearance will always be betrayed by our eyes, that faraway look in our eyes. On the other hand, no amount of dressing down can obscure a beautiful spirit.

The weak can never forgive.
Forgiveness is the attribute of the strong.
—*Mahatma Gandhi*

The finest retribution for being wronged is to not let the perpetrator's stupid or insane behavior occupy your mind and disturb your consciousness with a troubling lust for revenge. For vengeful thoughts easily become obsessive, and this obsession, once begun, will aggressively eat away at the fabric of your well-being.

Forgiveness is an active virtue that requires much strength and deliberation. Before we can forgive another we must first forgive ourselves, forgive ourselves for what we did, or did not, do, and so split the Gordian knot of guilt. Once we accomplish this, we can then set about relieving ourselves of the preoccupying feelings of resentment toward our malefactor.

All of this should be done with an eye toward keeping ourselves balanced, of not unmercifully succumbing to the moths of bitterness and vengeance. Of course, this does not mean you have to invite the malefactor to dinner, only that you absolve the actor, but without condoning the act.

*You know you've achieved perfection in design,
not when you have nothing more to add, but when you
have nothing more to take away.*
—Antoine de Saint-Exupéry

Seek not to add love to your heart, but to take hatred away.

Seek not to add peace to your mind, but to take confusion away.

Seek not to add beauty to your person, but to take ugliness away.

Subtract the illness and you have health.

Minus the sorrow and you have joy.

You cannot add one inch to the stature of the tree,

But you can remove the canopy that's preventing its highest growth.

Fulfillment

Men for the sake of getting a living forget to live.
—Margaret Fuller

We are an industrious species, spending the bulk of our time working. Indeed, as far as work is concerned, we are more like ants than apes. Like a colony of ants, we are highly organized and keep maddeningly busy. Unlike the great apes, we don't have an abundance of leisure time. Between the ages of five and sixty-five we spend the majority of our waking hours occupied with one task or another. This being the case, shouldn't we pursue fulfilling endeavors? Shouldn't our labors be purposeful and somewhat exhilarating rather than responsible drudgery, a burdensome chore?

Of course, we require food, clothing, and shelter and feel dutybound to provide these for our families; but still, shouldn't peace of mind, happiness, and a sense of personal accomplishment also be weighed in the balance? This is a question each of us needs to answer.

Be not forgetful to entertain strangers, for thereby some
have entertained angels unawares.
—Hebrews 13:1–2

Rare indeed in these isolating modern times do we even get the opportunity to entertain strangers, let alone angels. A weary traveler is not likely to alight at your door, as happened in the old days. The days of that kind of hospitality, even cordiality, are going, and we need to retrieve them.

Being hospitable and cordial is an essential part of human society. When basic courtesies fail, then distrust and violence are not far behind. Paramount to living peaceably on this ever-crowding planet are respect and proper manners.

Without a gracious affability we live in constant consternation and with an unhealthy disdain for our fellow man. So smile, and say "please" and "thank you," "good afternoon" and "good-bye," and engage in any of the other civilities that help maintain a civilized civilization.

The Guiding Voice Within

The soul's emphasis is always right.
—Ralph Waldo Emerson

Call it the angel on our shoulder or the spirit within, whatever it is that makes us go to the right when we wanted to go left deserves not only our thanks and praise but also our keen attention.

Who knows how many mishaps we've met along the way because we were not aware of its presence? And who knows how many missteps we've avoided because we *were* aware of its presence?

Quietly it speaks, and quietly we must listen, in order to hear its subtle prompting. Once prompted by this voice at the center of our being, we must, despite any objections, set our course accordingly. Otherwise, we will be sailing against the wind.

If the other person injures you, you may forget the injury;
but if you injure him you will always remember.
—*Kahlil Gibran*

When another hurts us we can forgive and forget, let bygones be bygones, and still get a decent night's sleep. Since it's in our best interest to let it go, we can, with a little effort, find an excuse for the offender's behavior. The mother was a drunk or the father was verbally abusive—the excuses usually fall along these lines, and we accept them on these lines.

But what happens when we are the ones who inflict the injury? What happens when our hands become sullied? Since deep down we know how feeble our excuses are, how unreasonable our reasons, our hands aren't cleansed so easily.

Indeed, the grime may be indelible, may remain an unsightly mark on our memory, a recurring haunting, which is why it is wise to tread softly on other people's feelings, to be wary of causing unnecessary heartache, to act without malice, and to do unto others only as we would have them do unto us.

We have just enough religion to make us hate,
but not enough to make us love one another.
        —Jonathan Swift

God's not a superstition, only the rituals that surround him are—
rituals based on the visions of a few highly developed spiritual
people. Once these visionaries' contemporaries run these insights
through the mill of interpretation, acculturation, and formulariza-
tion, which subsequent generations unthinkingly follow, you then
have the divisive superstitions of a modern religion.

Hedged about by their ritualistic worship of God, these religions tend to be exclusive rather than inclusive. A sense of the
Divine has always been, and so has the childish senselessness of
believing my God is better than your God. Yet if the original
seers and sages said anything at all, they said God is One, both
part and whole.

*Don't say you don't have enough time. You have exactly
the same number of hours per day that were given to
Helen Keller, Louis Pasteur, Michelangelo, Mother Teresa,
Leonardo da Vinci, Thomas Jefferson, and Albert Einstein.*
—H. Jackson Brown

Don't tell us anymore that you don't have enough time.
Time here. Time now.
It's your time here and now, forever and never again.
Take it. Live it.
Dance naked in your living room.
Sing soprano in the spring.
Walk across the park on your hands.
But don't say anymore that you don't have time.
Look up. Look down.
Stop and turn around.
Hold your breath.
Chase a butterfly.
Watch the entire sunset.
Everything and anything—just don't tell us you don't have time.
There will be time enough for no time.

We cannot change anything until we accept it.
Condemnation does not liberate, it oppresses.
—Carl Jung

Discounting of people out of hand seems to be growing more prevalent. Intolerance is gaining the day. What happened to the mature and cultivated way of dealing with those we differ with? Differences are the spices in what otherwise would be a rather bland stew. So, instead of reproach, why don't we approach; instead of denounce, why don't we start to listen? Otherwise, fear and misunderstanding prevail, and life becomes a series of futile arguments or summary dismissals, both of which lead to the tyranny of narrowness.

It is easier to love humanity as a whole
than to love one's neighbor.
—Eric Hoffer

Let's try living together. Now there's a novel idea. Forget living in peace and harmony and all that utopian jazz; let's just try living together. All of us have done it, have lived together with others; in fact, we're doing it now, living together: you, me, and everyone else you see. It's not so bad, trying at times, but not so bad— better than the alternative. What do you say? Now that we're all here, living in the same room so to speak, let's try living together. After all, the choices in the matter are quite limited.

He that will not apply new remedies
must expect new evils.
—Francis Bacon

That we should suffer for following our lust is inevitable. That we should become involved in unhappy relationships because we prefer rotten company to no company, this is understandable. But that we should bemoan our difficulties because of the choices we made with our eyes closed, this is unforgivable. It's not because the gods are aligned against us that we repeatedly find ourselves compromised in destructive relationships, but that we are misaligned, not balanced with our inner gyroscope. Instead of feeling sorry for ourselves and blaming fate, we should attempt to deliver ourselves from the dispositions of mind that repeatedly lead us to incompatibility and trouble.

The journey of a thousand miles begins with a single step.
—*Lao-tzu*

Maybe it's not too late; maybe it's never too late and each moment offers us a chance to be complete, like an elephant is complete or a violet is complete.

Sleepless, and spiritually undernourished, we are beginning to understand the full extent of the word *longing*, and to see the significance of those stories we were forced to read as children, the ones about men lost and crying out in a wilderness, some of whom never left their neighborhoods.

Now, we know what it means to be hollow of heart, that it's like a cave, a cold, dark, and desolate hole in an otherwise abundant mountain.

Perhaps what we don't know is that this mountain's ascending cliffs are speckled with a variety of evergreens, and that a mountain peak is there not only to be looked upon but also to be looked out from; and that, though difficult at times, this particular ascension requires no special gear, no rigs or ropes.

To reach the summit, you need only take the first step.

*The brain is a wonderful organ; it starts working
the moment you get up in the morning and does not stop
until you get into the office.*
—Robert Frost

Our consciousness, not unlike our home, is filled with the accumulated bric-a-brac of our lives. We have a basement filled with memories, a living room filled with present prospects, and a bedroom with dreams of the future, along with an attic filled with we're not quite sure what. Each day we find ourselves wandering through these various rooms, trying to find the string that will lead us out of this labyrinth. Even outdoors in the yard, even at the office, we remain fixed in the four walls of our consciousness, ever winding through the halls of our self-conscious thinking. This obsessive thinking morning, noon, and night engenders spiritual weariness and an internal discord and makes us feel for all the world like a person who lost his keys: agitated and not so sure what to do about it.

What to do about it? Good question. First we have to see the problem before we can see about a solution.

Consistency is the last refuge of the unimaginative.
—*Oscar Wilde*

Each new situation requires a new response. No sense always bringing yesterday's answers to today's questions. Only a hopeless bore completely and regularly conforms. Invariably, the unduly consistent find themselves facing throughout their lives similar problematic situations, to which they consistently respond inadequately. Old age becomes a wasteland of loneliness and bitterness for those who stubbornly refused to adapt, those that now can be forever heard saying, "In my day we didn't do . . ." or "In my day we did . . ." Remember, though the question may be the same, one year the answer may be yes, and the next, no.

DAY 25 ✦ Rhetoric

He who establishes his argument by noise and command
shows that his reason is weak.
—*Montaigne*

The man on the podium gesticulating wildly, talking loudly, authoritatively, and with much vehemence, of this person you should be suspect. Anyone that eager to convert others to his point of view usually stands on uncertain ground. A person who speaks the truth, speaks it passionately yet quietly, without fanfare and rhetoric, and without the slightest desire to convert anyone, this person should be listened to. Like an artist, a true prophet speaks because he must, not because he's trying to convert or convince. He is the fountain from which truth pours forth; it is for others to bring their thirst and their cups.

DAY 26 ✦ Being Prepared

A smooth sea never made a skillful mariner.
—English proverb

Certainly the English Channel can't be described as a smooth sea, and the English are notable mariners. To develop a skill or talent for something requires knowing how to handle the rough spots. If everything has been smooth sailing, you're sunk by the first unfavorable wind because of lack of preparation. A ready and able sailor knows the vicissitudes of the sea and accepts them. Without being reckless, a good sailor learns how to maneuver in a storm should one happen upon him. Not expecting one but being prepared for one, a true seaman knows how to ride out a storm, skillfully keeping the ship afloat by rolling with the waves. And there will always be waves.

No scriptures can make us religious.
We may study all the books that are in the world,
yet we may not understand a word of religion or God.
—*Swami Vivekenanda*

I may tell you that God resides in the tiniest leaf on a tree, or on the slopes of the grandest mountain, but if you know it not in your heart, what does it avail?

I may tell you that God inhabits the ant crawling on the forest floor, or the lion stalking on the savanna, but if you know it not in your heart, what does it avail?

I may tell you that God resounds in the echo of the dolphin, or in the cooing of the waves, but if you know it not in your heart, what does it avail?

I may tell you God speaks in the voice of your friend, and in the shout of your enemy, but if you know it not in your heart, what does it avail?

Absence diminishes little passions and increases great ones, just as the wind blows out a candle and fans a fire.
—*La Rochefoucauld*

To be absent requires someone or something to be absent from. A beloved's absence should fill rather than empty; it should fill us with passion and not empty us into loneliness. If it empties, this means we use our beloved's presence to fulfill ourselves, and thus absence finds us wanting. If it fills, this means our beloved is present within us, and thus absence finds us impassioned. The empty version in this scenario is a sign of neediness and insecurity, while the full version is a sign of wholeness and stability. Absence should make the heart grow fonder, not more despondent. Absence should inspire our love, not despoil our well-being. Clinging suffocates. Letting go liberates.

DAY 29 ✦ Discernment

If at first you don't succeed, try, try again. Then give up.
No use being a damned fool about it.
—W. C. Fields

Life is permeable, not impermeable. Life is flexible, not rigid. Life is tractable, not intractable. No use being a "Cool Hand Luke" when your stubborn persistence results only in the stockade and loss of freedom. A valiant effort can quickly degenerate into headstrong imbecility. So be resolute, but realistic; be determined, but practical; be purposeful, but sensible, and soon you will come to understand that giving up isn't necessarily synonymous with defeat—it can also be another kind of victory. Discernment suggests that it is wiser to end what can only be perilously and recklessly continued, especially if the reason for continuing is something so infantile as self-righteous stubbornness. As they say, "If you'll only walk away, you'll live to 'whatever' another day."

If the only tool you have is a hammer,
you tend to see every problem as a nail.
—*Abraham H. Maslow*

A foolish rich man considers all his problems in terms of money. He figures he can throw money at any problem and thereby solve it. And most of his problems are of a financial nature because he sees life on these terms.

Life appears to be the puppet and he the puppeteer until he comes face-to-face with a problem that defies a monetary solution, a real human problem like disease, death, or the ending of a relationship. Then he is at a loss; his money as worthless as paper, and his puppet unresponsive—a limp, wooden thing that can no longer be manipulated.

At such times, what he learns, and needs to learn, is a new perspective—another way of seeing and dealing with life and its many travails. With new eyes he finds new meaning.

Though I speak with the tongues of men and of angels, and have not love, I am become as sounding brass or a tinkling cymbal. . . .
—I Corinthians 13:1

Eloquent and wealthy, strong and healthy, but without love, you are a mere cipher, an empty vessel. If you can't love someone, at least love something. Be it a garden, a pet, a hobby, a vocation, or an art, have a love affair with something. Oddly enough, you may just find through loving something, that someone to love. Love, it seems, like music, is contagious. When you are filled with the notes of love, others can't help but hear and be moved by them.

DAY 32 ✦ Tradition

Tradition is a guide and not a jailer.
—W. Somerset Maugham

Used as a guide to establish the continuity of shared experience, many traditions are wonderful and useful. But other traditions are foolish, prejudicial beliefs that we soon grow accustomed to out of a false sense of loyalty to the past. Too often we are negatively bound by traditions.

We must take it upon ourselves to break the chains of custom when they become detrimental to our well-being. This is no mean feat as the manacles of tradition tie us firmly to our social routine, and to step outside long-established paths of behavior inspires rancor.

But to simply accept, whatever the cost, what is *now* simply because it *was* makes about as much sense as still sacrificing virgins to appease the sun god.

In order to continue to evolve as people we must on occasion shake free from the influence of hidebound convention.

What's in a Word?

Words divide us, actions unite us.
—Slogan of the Tupamaros

Chinese. Japanese. Irish. English. Indian. Pakistani. Slav. Croatian. American. Iraqi.

Atheist. Agnostic. Hindu. Christian. Muslim. Jew. Harmless words, no?

My country. Their country. My religion. Their religion. My neighborhood. Their neighborhood.

My house. Their house. My family. Their family. My person. Their person.

And this is the irreducible formula of words that causes the sorrow of the world.

It is seldom that liberty of any kind is lost all at once.
—*David Hume*

Like some insidious intestinal worm that slowly grows in our gut until finally and unsuspectingly we are overcome, so it is with the loss of liberty, both political and psychological liberty. Piecemeal, this is the way we lose our inner and outward freedom—one little bite at a time. Outwardly, restrictive laws are being passed every year, and inwardly the same thing is happening; each passing year finds us more mentally restricted, and we are the legislatures of this interior enslavement. We restrict ourselves by building up constraining psychological constructs until, imperceptibly, our inward liberty fails and we become but a walking opinion, a cadaver of beliefs. It takes open-minded awareness and discernment to not gradually cannibalize our liberty in this way. We must therefore be not just outwardly, but also inwardly, vigilant in the struggle to maintain the balance of our freedom. Political freedom is virtually meaningless without psychological freedom.

DAY 35 ◆ Eyes

All our souls are written in our eyes.
—Edmond Rostand

The eyes harbor all, harbor all that is woebegone and sad, and all that is joyous and happy in our souls. All that is courageous and forthright, and all that is fearful and dishonest, the eyes harbor all. The eyes have all that is loving and kind and all that is spiteful and inimical contained within their gaze. Both the tears of laughter and the tears of despair sluice from these windows. To be sure, the novel that is our life is being written in these evocative apertures, and nothing is sadder in all the world than a pair of inconsolable eyes, and nothing is happier than eyes gleaming with the poetry of love.

DAY 36 ✦ Learning

Iron rusts from disuse, stagnant water loses its purity,
and in cold weather becomes frozen; even so does
inaction sap the vigors of the mind.
—Leonardo da Vinci

Most of us never attend to any new subjects after we finish school. Sure, we watch television and go to the movies, and perhaps read the latest hit novel, but we rarely ever tackle an unfamiliar subject, and so don't set our minds ablaze with discovery. It is a demonstrable if obvious fact that when we are learning the synapses in our brain are vigorously firing, and that when we are idle they are sluggish. So, engage yourself mentally on occasion lest your mind become a dull and habitual thing barely conscious of its own rut.

As you well know, it's quite difficult to teach an old dog a new trick.

DAY 37 ✦ Optimism

Be an optimist—at least until they start moving
animals in pairs to Cape Canaveral.
—source unknown

A healthy optimism is the first ingredient in a successful endeavor. More often than not, the difference between boom or bust, winning or losing, hitting or missing, success or failure, hinges on attitude. To be confident and self-assured, as opposed to uncertain and uneasy, changes the entire aspect of an undertaking. Without some sense of positive expectation, of seeing the glass as half full, our lives become an oppressive mix of cynicism and bitterness.

Of course, this is not to suggest that we should walk around with rose-colored glasses. If the roof is caving in, the roof is caving in, and we better get a move on because a bright and sunny disposition will not stop its falling on our head. Nevertheless, to be optimistic until the evidence suggests otherwise bespeaks of a pure and knowing heart.

To ask the hard questions is simple.
—W. H. Auden

But to find the difficult answers is another matter entirely. Perhaps this is because there are no definitive answers as such, but only ways of living as different and varied as people themselves. We must find the curiosity and courage within ourselves to ask the hard questions and then have the passion to find the answers (if indeed there are any answers to the hard questions).

One thing is for sure, my answer is not your answer, and yesterday's answer may not suffice for today's question.

Inquire, and then inquire again, and know that sometimes the whispering wind may carry to you an answer or two.

Decay is inherent in all compounded things.
Strive on with diligence.
—Buddha

At first glance, we may find this idea depressing and cause for despair. Yet the truth of it is inescapable, and the inescapable truth fully grasped is never cause for despair, but for rejoicing. Thus we have the fully realized life of Buddha, who awakened himself to the ephemeral nature of life and found it not wanting but beautiful. Rather than being blighted by this idea of decay, he blossomed. Consequently and perhaps paradoxically, after over two thousand years this man's words have not at all decayed, but continue to be timely and have a deep impact on those who read them.

Love means the body, the soul, the life, the entire being.
We feel love as we feel the warmth of our blood,
we breathe love as we breathe air,
we hold it in ourselves as we hold our thoughts.
Nothing more exists for us.
—Guy de Maupassant

Romance, ah, but that word doth still sound sweetly sliding off the tongue!

If, at the moment, you should be lucky enough to be falling in love, go for it. Fall completely. Don't hold anything back. Be, for once, like a romantic poet and bask in the enchantment. Sing the Song of Solomon. Shower Aphrodite with gifts. Allow yourself the luxury of being exquisitely vulnerable.

At long last drink lustily from the cup of sensuality to the health and prosperity of twoness; to the potential for one to become two to make one again.

After all, it's not often that we're enabled to see the world with such clarity; not often we get to feel how marvelous this chaos we call life can be.

*A man who lives, not by what he loves but
what he hates, is a sick man.*
—*Archibald MacLeish*

A person I once knew would frequently watch evangelical television programs simply so he could fill himself with venom and spew it out at the screen: He would shout at the evangelists preaching on the television in front of him, "You phonies" . . . "Take down that phone number, you greedy thieves" . . . "You hypocrites, quit begging" . . . and on and on. He exulted in his hatred.

Admittedly, this is a somewhat mild if not amusing example, but an example nonetheless of the illness of hatred, the kind of hatred that drives some people's lives. If we're not careful we unwittingly store up hatred until it consumes and overtakes us, and before we know it loathing becomes our driving force. Obviously, living like this is antithetical to a happy and healthy life and serves only to abase the spirits of those so engaged. Be vigilant therefore, and don't let hated be the minister of your days.

DAY 42 ✦ Joy

The grand show is eternal. It is always sunrise somewhere;
the dew is never dried all at once; a shower is forever falling;
vapor is ever rising. Eternal sunrise, eternal dawn and gloaming,
on sea and continents and islands, each in its turn,
as the round earth rolls.
—John Muir

The fleeting glance of a stranger in a sidewalk café,

The glorious bursts of color caught in a cloud at sunset,

The multifoliate thoughts that fill and swell the head,

The changing faces of the wandering moon are all but drops in the living ocean,

But changing moments in this pageant called life; and yet abides in a clear pair of eyes,

In the spectral colors, in the silence between thoughts, and in the diurnal moon, a timeless joy.

No house should ever be on any hill or on anything.
It should be of the hill, belonging to it, so hill and house
could live together each the happier for the other.
—Frank Lloyd Wright

In the same way, we should not just be "in a relationship" but belong to it, not like we belong to a club, but like a flower belongs to the stem and is all the happier for it.

In the same way, we should not be just on this earth but of it and belong to it, and each of us has his or her place and should be all the happier for it.

We should be all the happier for it too if we felt like we belonged to our bodies and wore our skins well.

We would be all the happier for it too if we feel we are of the spirit and belong to it entirely.

Prayer does not change God, but changes him who prays.
—*Søren Kierkegaard*

Dialogue recorded at the prayer switchboard:

Operator: "God's mind has already been made up; sorry, but nothing you can say will change that. . . ."

Caller: "But . . . but, but please! I'm begging you! . . . did you remember to tell him that I would never again—"

Operator: "Yes, yes, I told him, but he'd already heard that one; in fact, he's heard them all . . . have a nice day."

The mind works in mysterious ways, and prayer is one of the ways it uses for self-transformation. Serious and humble prayer enables one to commune with the inner mysteries, to touch the very fabric of the soul. Not abstractly wanting and pleading, but earnestly searching and inquiring, this is prayer.

Advice is like snow; the softer it falls, the longer it dwells upon, and the deeper it sinks into the mind.
—Samuel Taylor Coleridge

The less forceful and judgmental, the better is the advice. Speak softly and throw away the big stick. Intelligent people tend to listen better when they're not being beaten with words. Declaim and you shall be ignored. Harangue and you shall be disregarded. Sermonize and you shall be disdained. Whereas if you speak earnestly and compassionately, showing concern for the one in need of counsel, being attentive to that person's uncertainty, then you will find a receptive audience, a serious listener. What you then say may be of some moment and given proper consideration. Otherwise, you are but a dog barking aimlessly in the night.

When love turns into dust,
money becomes the substitution.
—D. H. Lawrence

"I'm depressed; I think I'll go shopping." "My wife doesn't love me anymore; I think I'll go out and buy a new sports car." Maybe it's because we were given toys instead of answers when we felt troubled as children that we behave thus. But it's time to put away childish things and accept no substitutes. That love should turn to dust does not necessarily mean that we should turn into shoppers. Money as a substitute will buy you only depression and debt. Accept no substitutes. Put away childish things. Communicate, and you and your relationship will exfoliate; internalize and escape, and you and your relationship will be felled.

Remember also that "they are not long, the days of wine and roses."

Beauty is everywhere a welcome guest.
—*Johann Wolfgang von Goethe*

Should you walk today among a freshly blooming rose garden, would you feel at home with beauty, at ease with the awakening buds, deeply aware of their striking colors and poignant fragrances, aware of their very essence?

Should you walk today among a freshly blooming rose garden, would you discover what it takes to cultivate beauty?

Affection and consideration allow beauty to blossom, and once in bloom it will give of itself only one thing—the beautiful.

DAY 48 · Affection

Talk not of wasted affection; affection never was wasted.
—Henry Wadsworth Longfellow

What bounty affection is! How it soothes the soul of the
savage breast and transforms the uncreated into the
creative:
Spun by the loom of affection,
Her tenderness embraces me.
Wrapped in this silky thread
I am softened to places and days.
No longer distant and tomorrow,
Now, I weave the tapestry of moments,
An artisan for life.

*You've got to do your own growing, no matter
how tall your grandfather was.*
—*Irish proverb*

Those older and wiser than we may forewarn and admonish, explain and express to us the possible folly of a course of action we're intent on, but we embark nonetheless, because no advice will suffice for the living out of our own experiences. Our course of action may lead to darkness and despair, and those older and wiser than we may say "I told you so." Living on borrowed experience is not living at all—as if your insatiable hunger could ever be satisfied by a mere description of the banquet. You yourself must attend the festivities and partake of the repast; you must sample and taste the various offerings to appease your belly. This is not to say that you should be heedless of the sometimes sage advice of those older and wiser and make a pig of yourself, only that growing without experiencing your own growing pains is not on the menu.

When I dance, I dance; when I sleep, I sleep; yes, and when
I walk alone in a beautiful orchard, if my thoughts drift
to far-off matters for some part of the time, for some other part
I lead them back again to the walk, the orchard, to the
sweetness of this solitude, to myself.
—*Montaigne*

Our thoughts seem to incessantly "drift to far-off matters." Alas, even in the most exotic locales we can be back at the office in our troubled heads. To be "there" where you are wherever you are, in the orchard or on the road, may be the most arduous lesson life has to offer, and perhaps the most profoundly important. No doubt our minds love to drift, but do we notice this? Do we realize when we are struggling in a mental Ping-Pong match? Do we understand that when we are bouncing one thought off another we are missing the moment? If we do, we may yet lead ourselves back to the orchard.

You may forget with whom you laughed,
but you'll never forget with whom you wept.
—Arab proverb

Sorrow creates a deep bond between people. When you allow yourself to shed tears, to be vulnerable in the presence of another, you are making a lasting connection based on trust. This connection is not easily forgotten and should never be betrayed. Crying should never be dismissed as a sign of weakness, but rather embraced as a sign of the strength and courage to feel. It may not be too much of a stretch to say that a family that weeps together stays together.

*When I get a little money, I buy books. And if
there is any left over, I buy food.*
—*Erasmus*

Here we have in two short declarative sentences the passion for learning. Food for thought taking precedence over food for the stomach. Such admirable ardor for wisdom deserves our respect and emulation. Of course, in Erasmus' day books weren't as inexpensive and accessible as they are today, and therefore required more of a sacrifice to obtain.

Nonetheless, how many of us, even after grocery shopping, bother to buy books; or if we can't afford to buy them, then go to the library to borrow them for free? Stephen King and Tom Clancy might be good to pass a few diverting hours but they aren't sufficient to stretch the fibers of your mind. Find something that will stimulate your creative mind and get you to thinking.

Everything has been written about, and if it hasn't, it will be. So if you need information or knowledge, the means are available to you if you wish to avail yourself of them. The Internet itself can be used as one vast library, a library awaiting your fingertips. With so much knowledge accessible and available, is it not becoming harder and harder these days to excuse ignorance?

DAY 53 ✦ Honesty

Deception may work for a time, but the deceiver is always outed in the end. Especially when you consider that despite Herculean efforts, in the end, you cannot deceive yourself. Not to mention the prodigious memory required being a successful deceiver, along with the continuous stress living a lie must cause one. Besides, the deception game is not worth the candle, so why not make life easier and less apprehensive and simply tell the truth? Certainly a less fraudulent life means fewer misgivings and more freedom, less confusion and more self-esteem. If you so happen to be an expert in this macabre art of deception and have gotten yourself tangled in an unholy web of lies, the quickest and most efficient way to extricate yourself is by being honest now.

I am a human, and nothing human
is alien to me.
—Terence

Human beings daily commit monstrous acts, but they are human acts. Human beings daily engage in saintly and heroic acts, but these also are human acts. What the least of my brothers and sisters do and the best of my brothers and sisters do are human, all too human.

To say that a cruel and evil person is an animal is to disparage the animals. To say that a compassionate person is an angel is to diminish the compassionate nature of people. All that is of heaven and hell resides within our breasts. The difference is some act from the hell within and some act from the heaven within. Each of us has known and can conceive of both; hence the biblical injunctions against judging others.

DAY 55 ✦ Conscience

We are punished by our sins, not for them.
—Elbert Hubbard

Our transgressions against our own sense of morality carry their own punishments. When we engage in contrary behavior the ever-alert conscience is on hand to mete out justice. So it is that by our own actions we are both judged and chastised. Regret, self-recrimination, remorse, guilt, shame, are all so many wardens seeing to our sentence. Without this internal justice system life would be unbearably cruel and heartless. It's this "still small voice," this reliable censor, that does most to maintain whatever order we have in society.

A society is only as good as its conscience, and when that conscience is muted, there is chaos and barbarism.

DAY 56 ✦ Humor

Humor poses within its realm a magical quality for transformation. Despite feeling terribly sullen and humorless, we need only inadvertently come across something comical to find our mood altered, which is why laughter can be a powerful antibiotic for cold and gray days: a few hearty giggles and we remarkably find our gloominess turned into cheerfulness. Even at those times when we try to reject its influence outright, humor may nonetheless overtake us, and we then find ourselves laughing in spite of ourselves. This seems to demonstrate that some things are objectively funny, that "funny" is funny, circumstances notwithstanding. So laugh while the laughing is good, for as the saying goes, "He who laughs last lasts."

*An animal needing something knows how much
it needs; the man does not.*
—Democritus

A bird knows precisely the size nest required to safely and comfortably accommodate its brood. A bear knows exactly when, and for how long, to hibernate. An elephant drinks its fill from a water hole, and then moves on. But a man, a man has trouble buying socks, let alone fulfilling his most fundamental needs. The knowledge we possess regarding our own needs can be summed up in one word—*more*. More of this and more of that, and when we've had enough, just a little bit more—more of things but less of life. To have more or not to have more, that is the question. And if the answer is to have more, keep in mind that, nowadays, it does take an outrageous fortune.

Start by doing what's necessary; then do what's possible,
and suddenly you are doing the impossible.
—Saint Francis of Assisi

If we can discover what it is we need to do, then we will see that it is possible, possible because it is necessary. Yet the difficulty lies in that first step, the discovery. Mainly we do not do what is necessary for not knowing what is necessary to do. Once we see what needs to be done we've conquered the greatest obstacle. Then when we begin doing what is necessary the possibilities grow and grow until finally what we would have thought at the outset to be impossible is mysteriously at hand. This is why it is important to begin by doing only what's necessary in the beginning so as not to give up before you even get started.

We all indulge in the strange, pleasant process called thinking,
but when it comes to saying, even to someone opposite, what
we think, then how little we are able to convey!
—Virginia Woolf

How many times have you rehearsed in your head what you will say to someone, only to find when you're face-to-face with that person that what you thought to say disappears into confused stammering? Abstracting in your mind can never meet the reality. The person's reactions will always, despite every contingency, be such to throw you off balance, to make you say differently what it was you so earnestly wanted to say. The few times we speak from the soul are the few times we convey truly and can be understood.

Try less-rehearsed talking and more speaking from the spirit and you may find a new clarity of expression.

*Ultimately, the only power to which man should aspire
is that which he exercises over himself.*
—Elie Wiesel

Power gives us a sense of security, and we all like to feel secure. Wielding power, we feel in control, and we all like to feel in control. Yet the more power we wield over others, the less secure and in control we actually are. This paradox leads those in positions of power to treachery and abuse, sometimes to the most horrific abuses imaginable. A wise man therefore does not aspire to such a confused and uncertain position. Concerned with self-mastery, a wise man possesses another kind of power entirely, an inner radiance that rejects all outward displays of authority.

*Parents can only give good advice or put them
on the right paths, but the final forming of a person's
character lies in their own hands.*
—Anne Frank

Our forebears have passed on to us an abundance of good advice;
enough good advice, one would think, to make our choices clear,
our lives easy. But our choices aren't always clear, and—Lord
knows!—our lives aren't so easy. So what is it? Individuality, that's
what it is. Our individual temperament and the times dictate how
we will act, and our actions go a long way toward forming our
character and reforming the times. One daughter may listen to her
parent's good advice, while her sister ignores it and her brother
implements it too late. Anyway, what was good advice to the
grandparents may not necessarily be so to the grandchildren.

Each to his or her own bed goes.

We are shaped and fashioned by what we love.
—*Johann Wolfgang von Goethe*

Everyone comes with strings attached, but some come with ropes, nooses with which, if we're not careful, we may just get hanged. If you're so inclined in love to repeatedly play the knight in shining armor or the nursemaid, you may wish to reconsider the consequences of trying to be Cupid's defender and savior. The hopelessly neurotic and needy beloved may yet be more than you bargained for. Your chivalry or your proclivity for mothering— whichever the case may be—may not be equal to rescuing your loved one from troubles. In other words, your assumed strength may not be as strong as his or her obvious weaknesses. And in such an affair, you may just end up as aggrieved and disordered as the one you so nobly tried to save. So take care that you don't willingly confuse pity with love and defiantly set out to resolve another's neuroses, for this type of arrogance can exact a heavy price.

To love is to be vulnerable.
—*C. S. Lewis*

We can both love and be vulnerable, or lock ourselves in a closet and have someone shove food and water under the door. To be alive is to be vulnerable. Avoiding heartache by shutting yourself off does not only you, but also life, a great disservice. So you've been jilted, scorned, hurt, betrayed—what of it? Haven't you also been loved, desired, and happy? Forget the martyred-lover syndrome and get back into the fray. Every time, this is one game that's worth the candle.

We ought to do good to others as simply as a horse runs,
or a bee makes honey, or a vine bears grapes season after
season without thinking of the grapes it has borne.
—*Marcus Aurelius*

Goodness toward others should be natural and effortless, not forced and constrained. In the main, a kind act should be done instinctively, without deliberation. Certainly, the greatest acts of goodness are undertaken without thoughts of personal advantage. Beware the self-righteous do-gooder who has a well-wrought plan for your well-being, as his primary concern is usually his own gain and gratification.

Discernible by its vitality and freshness, goodness is a dynamic inner quality that flows naturally from its source like a mountain spring. Its effluence can ever be drawn upon and never be diminished.

Season after bloody season goodness triumphs.

Blessed are the merciful,
for they will be shown mercy.
—Matthew 5:7

We tend to get as good as we give:
Our forbearance makes others forbearing of us.
Our sympathy pays sympathetic dividends.
Forgiveness of others allows us to be forgiving of ourselves.
Grace bestowed is graciousness received.
Kindness reaps its own kind.
Commiseration begets compassion.
Goodwill breeds goodness.
Charity given is generosity received.

Since things seem to be arranged thus, why not number ourselves among the blessedly merciful?

DAY 66 ✦ Action

Do you want to know who you are? Don't ask. Act!
Action will delineate and define you.
—*Witold Gombrowicz*

Character can be best assessed in action. To obtain a true reading of the barometer of your soul you must be aware of yourself in relationship: how you handle yourself with people, how you deal with things and places and various situations. Such active awareness gets you in touch with who you actually are, as opposed to who you think you are. Oftentimes we consider ourselves as being one way when we are actually another. We may think we are patient when in fact we are impatient, as we may easily ascertain if we observe our level of frustration when we find ourselves waiting in a long line at the market. To be sure, since we won't fix what we don't consider in disrepair, such real-time observation of ourselves is an indispensable means of seeing whatever problems may exist. Without a proper diagnosis, a remedy is unlikely.

The wise man always throws himself on the side of his assailants.
It is more his interest than it is theirs
to find his weak point.
—*Ralph Waldo Emerson*

Our antagonists can be our greatest allies in the war of self-discovery. Who better than our detractors to show us our faults? Many times there is some truth hidden in their bias. So it behooves us to find out if there is any merit in their antipathy. If we listen only to the praise of friends and not also to the criticism of adversaries, our growth will be stunted. Every face, benign or malignant, can and should be used as a looking glass into our own state of being. Without such an all-inclusive panorama we may miss unsightly blemishes that could otherwise be removed.

In everyone's life, at some time, our inner fire goes out.
It is then burst into flame by an encounter with another
human being. We should all be thankful for those people
who rekindle the inner spirit.
—*Albert Schweitzer*

A friend, a family member, an acquaintance, a person in the street, a new love—somehow, sometime, somewhere we fortuitously meet that person who reinvigorates us. These encounters number among the delightful mysteries of life and cannot be forced. The best you can do is not allow your inner fire to be completely extinguished. If you can keep even the slightest flicker alive in your breast, then such encounters will not be lost on you. Otherwise, you can sit at the foot of a master wielding a flame-thrower to no avail.

If only in our thoughts, these torches in the night deserve our heartfelt thanks and appreciation.

Where no wood is, there the fire goeth out: so where
there is no talebearer, the strife ceaseth.
—Proverbs 26:20

Keep confidential the confidences bequeathed to you. Do not
assume because you consider a matter trivial that you can break
another's trust in you with impunity. Trust is a noble and steadfast
quality measured by its consistency of application, and once betrayed, it is extremely difficult to redeem. Blessed are the trustwor-
thy and equally blessed are those who trust. Respect and honor
such blessedness and your life will be rich with the esteem and
friendship of many. Otherwise, cry wolf at your own peril.

In affairs both grand and small it is wise to be unconditionally
credible and dependable.

No greater thing is created suddenly, any more than a bunch
of grapes or a fig. If you tell me that you desire
a fig, I answer you that there must be time.
Let it first blossom, then bear fruit, then ripen.
—*Epictetus*

An overnight success is usually forgotten by early afternoon.

People desire success but they don't want to pay the dues. Success in any field of endeavor requires hard work; not only hard work but fortitude: the courage to overcome nagging doubts and the ability to handle setbacks with equanimity.

Michelangelo was said to have apprenticed in a stone quarry. He didn't just wake up one morning and sculpt *David*. Behind the story of every great artist you will find equal parts natural ability and dedication to the craft.

Forget these illusory notions of instant success and get to work.

*Modern man thinks he loses something—time—when he does
not do things quickly. Yet he does not know what to do
with the time he gains—except kill it.*
—*Erich Fromm*

Time, especially television time, can weigh heavy on our hands.
So many new gadgets—computers, cell phones, pagers, microwaves, fax machines—to speed things up mean so much more
time that we don't know what to do with.

Granted, if your job is to make widgets, you'll of course want
the fastest widget maker possible so you don't have to put in any
burdensome overtime at the widget factory. But the question still
remains about what to do with our free time.

Suppose, for a moment, you were the master of your own
time and could arrange your day as you pleased, having no "re-
sponsibilities" whatsoever. Would you be equal to such freedom?
How long do you think it would take—a month, six months, a
year—before you were catatonic from boredom?

What then, may I ask, is the rush? Where are we rushing?

Rather than do things quickly and poorly, why not do them
more carefully and skillfully and thus earn our free time with work
well done?

I tore myself away from the safe comfort of certainties through
my love for truth—and truth rewarded me.
—Simone de Beauvoir

We fit easily into our comfort zone, and there we remain, stable and secure, but utterly bored. Without making friends with the new and challenging, we extinguish the flame of passion.

Hopelessly revolving through the door of our habits we begin to languish, and this can lead to our taking drastic measures, such as suddenly and inexplicably leaving family and friends to go in search of the Sasquatch.

Before you find yourself so weary and frustrated that you're willing to do something rash and absurd, begin exploring, for the love of truth and the thrill of discovery, those mental certainties you've so faithfully constructed. Tear down those walls and you will be rewarded with a renewed vigor and zest for life. And, just think, this can happen without your having to aimlessly search the Pacific Northwest for extra-large footprints!

DAY 73 ✦ Mother Nature

Only after the last tree has been cut down,
Only after the last river has been poisoned,
Only after the last fish has been caught,
Only then will you find that money cannot be eaten.
—*Cree proverb*

Recently, I had occasion to talk with a neighbor who had just returned from a nine-mile hike through a forest. By way of small talk, I asked, "Did you see any wildlife?"

"Yeah, a bird," she said.

"What! . . . A bird? Just a bird? . . . That's it?"

"Yep," she said matter-of-factly.

"What was it, a pigeon?" I asked.

She smiled and said, "No, some sort of sparrow."

A sparrow! A nine-mile hike and all she saw was a sparrow. How depressing! Admittedly, wildlife can be quite elusive, especially when a large group of noisy people are about . . . but one sparrow after nine miles, a single solitary bird—that's ridiculous. What poverty!

This anecdote illustrates why it is important for us to continue to support, as best we can, conservation efforts.

After the years of abuse, now more than ever do we need to keep faith with nature.

DAY 74 ◆ Faith

*The majority of mankind is lazy-minded, incurious,
absorbed in vanities, and tepid in emotion, and is therefore
incapable of either much doubt or much faith.*
—T. S. Eliot

Let's talk about faith. Not blind faith, but a wide-eyed assurance in our own spiritual center.

To awaken to the loyalty and fidelity of our deeper purpose, surely this is something of incalculable value and worthy of consideration.

Surely this type of faith is of paramount importance.

Without it, we slip too easily into cynicism and despair, and often remain there unaware. With it, we find our way in the rugged and uncertain terrain of trouble and travail. Without it, we are blocked. With it, we may remove mountains.

So why not, if we haven't already, take a chance on trust, on ourselves, and on that natural faith that sleeps inside, true but untried?

Take the leap; you may just be surprised at the expanse of your wings.

DAY 75 ◆ History

*History is the version of past events that people
have decided to agree upon.*
—Napoléon

Or disagree, as the case may be. History is only as accurate as
the historian who transcribes it. Look at your own past and see
how you've revised and reinterpreted events in the light of new
experience. Everything that was is only what it seems now. Never
will past events be answered completely and finally in the present.
The facts may stay the same but their interpretations will vary
with time. Generations choose the past best suited to their present. Knowing this, we may better understand the nature of our
own development and that of our contemporaries.

DAY 76 ✦ Money

A rich man is nothing but a poor man with money.
— W. C. Fields

No one is born rich, all are born penniless.

No mother's milk can be gilded, and so the prince and the pauper are interchangeable. Children would just as soon play with a stone as a diamond. Nevertheless, sooner rather than later we find ourselves possessed with a desire for wealth.

We play the lottery and dream. We grow envious of our neighbor's new car. We come to daydream about the happiness that would be ours if we just had the right amount of money. After all, it's so much easier to put the burden of change on our finances rather than on ourselves.

To consider every financial gain as a spiritual gain is a deception that has ruined many lives. Whether you live in a mansion on a hill or in a rural cottage, sorrow is sorrow and happiness is happiness and no amount of money will change how they feel.

A man is not idle because he is absorbed in thought.
There is visible labor and there is invisible labor.
—*Victor Hugo*

Is it idleness to be so absorbed as to be able to construct in language the exquisite detail of the hauntingly beautiful Notre-Dame Cathedral? Surely it's not, but a laborious work of skill and imagination akin to the physical labor of hauling and laying brick.

Creativity requires an inward immersion that can be as exhausting and challenging as any manual labor; indeed, an artist may feel just as worn out as a bricklayer after such immersions.

An artist does need idle time to converse with the Muses. Such time enables him to replenish his creative forces and begin again the painstaking delivery of his work. Without these periods of germination nothing will sprout; thus they are essential. Best, therefore, not to chide yourself too severely for downtime since this is when the seeds of your next endeavor are being sown.

It's only words . . . unless they're true.
—David Mamet

Our entire intellectual psychology is built upon words. A limited vocabulary means a limited range of expression. While words used to describe the virtues of purchasing a toaster oven may be meaningless, words that possess the bite of truth can and oftentimes do have a powerful effect. *(Sticks and stones may break my bones but words of truth can forever change me.)* Which is precisely why listening is such an important skill. By listening properly we can distinguish the profound from the prosaic, the meaningful from the trivial. In an age when words like *love* and *enlightenment* are used to sell soft drinks, listening with discernment takes on an added significance.

However, never daunted, I will cope with adversity in
my traditional manner . . . sulking and nausea.
—Tom K. Ryan

While sulking and nausea may not be the ideal responses to adversity, they are responses nonetheless, and sometimes they are the only responses our body will allow. To be doubled over in anguish is not an uncommon coping response. In a storm, any shelter will do. However, to use such methods relentlessly and to carry them on beyond their appointed hour is self-indulgent and pitiful. If it's sympathy you're after, such histrionics cut an unsympathetic figure. Using grief to posture and pose is self-defeating, as any actor who has ever overplayed his part can tell you. Only if you're playing the role of Desdemona should you insufferably carry on night in and night out like a whimpering dog. Otherwise, let your grief run its proper course, and don't make of it an enduring role to which you desperately cling.

DAY 80 ✦ Anger

When angry, count to four;
when very angry, swear.
—Mark Twain

Taught since childhood that anger is a shameful emotion, some of us keep all our anger bottled up inside, which makes about as much sense as keeping termites in a wooden jar. Repressed anger will eat you alive inside.

Whether it's called indignation or wrath, both saint and sinner experience anger, the difference being in the quality and kind of its expression. One may speak out resolutely and eloquently about fools who persist in their folly while the other may lash out in a violent and destructive rage. Needless to say, the former is a healthy and reasonable way to express anger and the latter is an unhealthy and unreasonable way to express anger. If you number yourself among the angered that lash out and then feel bitterly ashamed of yourself, instead of swearing never again to get angry—which, as you well know, does not and will not ever work—consider the way you manifest your anger. Count to four or forty, swear, wring your hands, scream if you must, anything but this continued violent acting out at the expense of the innocent.

The bitterest tears shed over graves are for words
left unsaid and deeds left undone.
—Harriet Beecher Stowe

Many times we consider too late what a brief candle life can be and then we are left with self-reproach and regrets for those words not spoken and kindnesses not done. Before that unexpected wind appears to blow out the light of the loves in your life, be sure they know what they've meant to you.

Thank your mother and father for what they did by saying, "I love you"; absolve your mother and father for what they did not do by saying, "I love you."

Forgive yourself and then tell your spouse you tried your best to do right by him or her and can only hope you didn't fall too short by saying, "I love you."

As difficult as such expressions of love and gratitude may be for some of us right now, it is not nearly so difficult as living will be with the feeling in our hearts and the words on our lips but no one left to say them to.

*Although the world is full of suffering,
it is full also of the overcoming of it.*
—Helen Keller

I don't know about you, but I'm properly tired of trying to overcome everything. Enough already, and let it come. What will be will be. Enough of this incessant struggling to beat and defeat, to conquer and win. The best we can be is equal to our suffering and not superior to it, because the things in life that truly matter can't be conquered, only understood. Besides, to the victor of the battle may just go the spoiling of the soul, and in constantly bettering yourself you may just best yourself. Relax, for we seem to be only given that which we can handle.

DAY 83 • Ignorance

I don't have any solution, but I certainly admire the problem.
—Ashleigh Brilliant

"I don't know . . . I just don't know." Aren't these words refreshing to hear? Too many people these days too much of the time these days think they know everything these days. Afraid of appearing ignorant, they stupidly speak out of turn. If someone should ask you a question and you don't know or are uncertain of the answer, count to ten before you speak and then don't say anything. This seems to be very sound advice, but since sound advice these days is generally summarily ignored, we can only hold fast to our sense of humor.

Noise proves nothing.
Often a hen who has merely laid an egg
cackles as if she had laid an asteroid.
—Mark Twain

Now that would be something to shout from the rooftops, a hen that laid an asteroid. Otherwise, it's probably best not to shout from the rooftops, as you may go hoarse for want of getting an audience.

As we tend to know ourselves better than we are credited with, we can quickly see through these self-inflated boasters, these epic braggarts who cry high and low their own praises and will doubtless have trouble keeping quiet even in the grave. And what does all their noise prove? It proves nothing, save that they're noisy, and that some days are longer than others.

"Silence is golden" and "All is vanity" and never the twain shall meet.

DAY 85 ✦ Beautification

A man should hear a little music, read a little poetry,
and see a fine picture every day of his life,
in order that worldly cares may not obliterate
the sense of the beautiful which God
has implanted in the human soul.
—*Johann Wolfgang von Goethe*

Beauty, the early-morning laughter of birds or a single elm standing on the crest of a hill glazed in the colors of dusk. Maybe these images don't mean anything to you. No matter. What about a congenial smile brightening the afternoon face of a pretty passerby? Or a clear thought on a clear evening? No. Well, it still doesn't matter, for surely something of beauty will occur to you today.

In my hut this spring, there is nothing—there is everything!
—Sodo

Anyone who has ever been filled with the fertile aura of spring knows this feeling. Everything seems both insignificant and magnificent, both worthless and priceless. In the fullness of spring things once regarded with the pride of possession are now looked upon with a certain detachment that makes them seem at once trivial and vital.

If you allow it, all that burgeoning life, all that flowering and arising that is spring can fill your breast with delight and can inspire you with an especially keen awareness, an awareness that sees the proper place and value of everything and realizes that nothing in and of itself really matters overmuch save for the fact that taken altogether that's all there is.

DAY 87 ♦ Listening Creatively

I like to listen.
I have learned a great deal from listening carefully.
Most people never listen.
—*Ernest Hemingway*

Does any of us listen properly? Have we heard the birds singing in the early morning, in the late afternoon? Have we heard recently the wind in the leaves, the wind through our hair? What about the sound of our own breathing, of our own thinking—that constant noise in our heads?

True listening is the gateway to understanding. If we can listen to what is going on within us and around us, listen without constantly judging, comparing, and contrasting, but quietly, deeply listen, then the process of creative learning begins. Give it a try. Drop your preoccupations, and spend some time listening to the diversity of sounds, the music of insight.

There is nothing more notable in Socrates
than that he found time, when he was an old man,
to learn music and dancing,
and thought it time well spent.
—Montaigne

To let go into the music, to dance, to spin and turn and sway as the sounds resound in your bones, to feel your feet grow light-hearted as they sweep you along to the rhythm of the music, is time well spent for young or old, philosopher or fool.

Like music and its endless variations, learning is an endless process, one that we should embrace throughout our lives. Nothing is more laudable than to live lyrically, to make of our lives a continuous song of experience.

DAY 89 ✦ Ways and Means

Men judge us by the success of our efforts.
God looks at the efforts themselves.
   —*Charlotte Brontë*

People in general are more concerned with ends than means—
one usually asks the final score of the game, not how well each
team played—but means and ends are inseparable. In the world
of the spirit, intent is all-important. Being results-oriented, overly
keen for the payoff, we give scant consideration to the means.
Keeping in mind the life experiences that suggest that the Karma
of life will repay in kind our selfless actions based on pure motives,
as well as our selfish actions concerned only with the payoff, we
might well attend more carefully to the means to our ends.

*. . . be patient toward all that is unsolved in your heart and try
to love the questions themselves. . . . Live the questions now.
Perhaps you will then gradually, without noticing it,
live along some distant day into the answer.*
—Rainer Maria Rilke

Each day it would behoove us to set aside some time for reflection, some time to digest the experiences we've consumed. Without such reflective moments our lives remain unresolved, and we grow more and more anxious and the questions become more and more perplexing. Contemplation gives the mind the time not only to discover the questions but also to work itself through to whatever answers there may be.

Ye must leave righteous ways behind,
not to speak of unrighteous ways.
—Buddha

Over time, indifference and apathy have a chilling effect on our own morality. Once we begin to care less and less, to grow jaded, a part of the goodness that was once innately ours also grows careless and jaded, and we may find ourselves doing and saying things we at one time would have found objectionable.

Amid all the senseless violence we are forever being bombarded with, and the seemingly incorrigible nature of the delinquent, we can easily fall silent in a stupor of moral apathy. Yet such a response is self-defeating, as it is a misstep in the direction of the "if you can't beat 'em, join 'em" attitude, and a stumble in that direction is not only an offense to your own dignity but also sends you headlong down the road to your own debasement.

Against all odds, keep in you burning the flames of goodness and integrity.

DAY 92 ✦ Security

If daily we remind ourselves of the fragility, insecurity, and wonderful unpredictability of life, then we are, paradoxically, graced with a sense of well-being, of internal freedom, a freedom that provides us with a deep regard for love. Otherwise, in our craving for security, we become anxious and clingy, and thereby lose—in our efforts to hold tight—this tremendous life-affirming energy called love. This is why it is vitally important to realize the transitoriness of life, for then we are capable of loving anew each day.

DAY 93 ✦ Living

There is no cure for birth and death
save to enjoy the interval.
—George Santayana

Obviously! But sometimes we need the obvious brought to our attention, because the obvious has a sneaky way of hiding itself. Besides, who, if asked, would want a cure for birth or death? No one, to be sure, but an extremely bitter or an extremely foolish person. Let's enjoy the interim, for, as far as anyone has been able to ascertain, the interim is all we've got. Birth and death will take care of themselves.

Pain and Pleasure

Look for a long time at what pleases you, and for
a longer time at what pains you.
—Colette

Most of us strive for pleasure while doing our best to disregard pain. Yet, do what we may, the pain is always there, because pain and pleasure are intimately linked—pain being complement of pleasure. Thus, it is in our best interest to examine them closely. Upon examination, we may find that a good deal of what pleases and pains us comes to us via acquired habits. Upon examination, we may begin to see that what pleases and pains us has been stamped into our minds at an early age.

Love and you shall be loved.
—*Ralph Waldo Emerson*

Give and you shall receive—"Love and you shall be loved"—Speak and you shall be spoken to—"Love and you shall be loved"—Listen and you shall hear—"Love and you shall be loved"—Touch and you shall feel—"Love and you shall be loved"—Smile and you shall be smiled upon—"Love and you shall be loved"—Be friendly and you shall earn a friend—"Love and you shall be loved"—Be considerate and you shall be considered—"Love and you shall be loved"—Be compassionate and you shall know compassion—and never forget, always remember—"Love and you shall be loved," "Love and you shall be loved."

DAY 96 ✦ Complaining

If all our misfortunes were laid in one common heap
whence everyone must take an equal portion,
most people would be contented to take
their own and depart.
—Socrates

A day is not complete without hearing someone complaining of his or her lot. Everyone has problems. This is a fact. So why do we spend so much time belaboring to others our difficulties? Wouldn't our energy be better spent on understanding our self and all the problems that go with this self? Moaning is not a cure for any ailment that I'm aware of. Surely, most of us aren't as bad off as we think, or as we would like others to think.

Luck affects everything, let your hook always be cast.
In the stream where you least expect it,
there will be fish.
—Ovid

Life's vagaries are many. Chance and mischance.

Luck comes knocking but we don't hear it, for the television is too loud. Then luck slips quietly away—takes a stroll down the street and knocks at another door. Here it finds an alert, patient person who cordially opens the door and says, "I've been expecting you." Together they enjoy some wine and mahimahi, talking like old friends.

He has half the deed done who has made a beginning.
—*Horace*

A difficult one, this. Indeed, I don't know where to begin . . . how to start . . . what to say . . . I've spent ten whole minutes (six hundred seconds) simply staring at the page trying to come up with a significant interpretation, a profound sentence encapsulating the entire depth and breadth of this quotation . . . Now I've got it—Just begin!

DAY 99 ✦ Staying Current

Let us not look back in anger, or forward with fear,
but around in awareness.
—*James Thurber*

Observation is the true temple of understanding. Looking too much before and after lends itself to frustration and anxiety. Imagine, for a moment, how difficult a leisurely stroll around the block would become if, when you weren't turning around, you were looking far ahead. Certainly, if nothing else, walking thus would impede your journey. In the same way, overthinking the past and constantly worrying about the future will impede your journey. The hum of the present is lost to us for the drone of the past and the hiss of the future. Attend, therefore, to what's at hand; admire, then, what's under you nose; regard, if you will, the lay of the land, and in this way the continuous movement of the present becomes your greatest ally.

*A morning glory at my window satisfies me more
than the metaphysics of books.*
—Walt Whitman

One can picture Walt Whitman, with his shaggy gray beard, disheveled hair, and bold, laughing eyes looking out his kitchen window at a morning glory, gazing intently at it, seeing the poetry in that brilliant flower.

Books have their place. Metaphysics has its place. Neither of them, though, can replace the quickened pulse of beauty revealed. Beauty is always a surprise; it opens to us unexpectedly, suddenly. Too much time spent studying, thinking, may obscure the revelations of beauty. In truth, all we require is a morning glory at our window and the sense(s) to appreciate it for beauty to be born within.

DAY 101 ✦ Spirit

*The nature of God is a circle of which the center is everywhere
and the circumference is nowhere.*
—*Empedocles*

Spirit pervades all. Spirit in matter and the immaterial.
Spirit here and spirit there.
You show spirit . . . The spirit within . . . This is a spiritual
place.
A spirit flew through the house. It was a spirited debate.
Drink some spirits. She is spiritual; he is spiritual; they are
spiritual.
She is in bad spirits; he is in bad spirits; they are in bad spirits.
Spirit here and spirit there.
Spirit pervades all; all is spirit.
Spirit here, spirit there, spirit everywhere, including nowhere.

DAY 102 ◆ Merit

The nobler the truth or sentiment,
the less imports the question of authorship.
—Ralph Waldo Emerson

Immediately upon entering the museum we want to know who painted the picture. If we've heard of him, it's a good picture; if not, we're not so sure until someone who has heard of him sets us straight on the matter. And so it goes with these quotations. If Emerson said it, it must be good, but if I've never heard of James Dewar, I'll skip that one. But is that truly what's important, the fame and reputation of the artist or writer, or the actual work in front of your eyes? Yes, your eyes—not someone else's. Not a scholar's or a critic's, but your brown or blue or green or hazel or gray or violet eyes. Surely the answer is in the reaction of those, your pupils.

You can't cross the sea merely by standing and staring at the water.
Don't let yourself indulge in vain wishes.
—*Rabindranath Tagore*

Thinking about the journey is not the journey. Simply reading a map will not get you there. The roads and byways are many and vast, and you can't travel on a symbol. The description of an elephant is not the elephant. One must put away the guide and make a beginning, even if it's an uncertain and difficult beginning. Whatever journey you have not begun, whether it be an inward or an outward journey, consider now taking that all-important first step.

Better to light one small candle than to curse the darkness.
—*Chinese proverb*

Problems fester and spread when left untended. We suffer more because we fail to apply a balm, take a curative for what ails us. When our tooth aches, we go to the dentist. When our spirit aches, what do we do? Do we take action, take steps to understand why we are suffering, or do we curse our fate and look for an immediate distraction?

Each of us has within the darkness, the candle, and the match. Strike the match, touch it to the wick, and so light your own way.

What you possess in the world will be found at the day
of your death to belong to someone else.
But what you are will be yours forever.
—Henry Van Dyke

Our possessions start out innocently enough, but quickly they end up possessing us. How attached we grow to our houses, cars, appliances, and all the material bric-a-brac accumulated in this life of accumulation! We become mad, irate, and sometimes even irrational when these things are damaged or threatened.

He who dies with the most toys does *not* win, as Midas did not win. Slick cars, fancy suits and dresses, diamonds and jewels, checkbooks and portfolios, these things cannot be taken with you.

You are not they and they are not you. Your personal deliverance is made of other stuff entirely.

DAY 106 ✦ Death

*Death is as sure for that which is born
as birth is for that which is dead.
Therefore grieve not for what is inevitable.*
—*Bhagavad Gita*

Death remains a haunting specter within, a black demon with a pitchfork that scares us out of living. Follow the tunnel of any fear and it will always lead to the dark cave of death. Fear, in its various forms, stems from the fear of dying.

"Lay your sleeping head, my love, faithless on my arm . . ." is the attitude we should adopt toward dying. After all, death is our birthright, and the handmaiden of beauty and creativity. So, let's live today, for tomorrow and tomorrow and tomorrow continue mysteriously and the unknown unavoidable end doesn't stop for fear.

It is not only for what we do that we are held responsible,
but also for what we do not do.
—Molière

The incomplete thought, the word left unexpressed, the dream not followed, the love withheld are as much ours as our limbs. These thoughts and deeds left incomplete can lead to the deepest sorrows, the profoundest regrets. It is important, therefore, that as responsible human beings we come to realize this truth, and begin to complete the thought, express the word, fulfill the kindness, and follow the dream—and love, most important of all, that we begin to properly love.

There is nothing stronger in the world than gentleness.
—Han Suyin

Lava flowing gently, yet inexorably, creates islands atop oceans;
Winds blowing breezily sculpt the greatest mountains;
Streams quietly cascading become the grandest rivers;
Elephants leisurely walking make the longest roads;
And the sun gently shining sustains the most varied life.

A musician must make music, an artist must paint, a poet must write,
if he is to be ultimately at peace with himself.
What one can be, one must be.
—Abraham Maslow

Dust off your guitar, dig out your old canvas, start your journal again, reawaken the sleeping artist within you. Of one thing I'm convinced, and that is that each person possesses a talent that needs to be cultivated and expressed in order for that person to be complete. Much of our restlessness and destructive behavior stems from our lack of artistic expression.

Creativity is a way to freedom from the tyranny of the self. Discover your innate artistic ability and practice it, and the shape and feel of the world will metamorphose in front of your very eyes.

A spider spins and weaves its silken web, a bird constructs its twig cathedral, a termite shapes its earthen mountain, a gazelle dances exuberantly its ceremonial dance, and a painter paints.

Do not believe in anything simply because you have heard it. Do not believe in anything simply because it is spoken and rumored by many. Do not believe in anything simply because it is found written in your religious books. Do not believe in anything merely on the authority of your teachers and elders. Do not believe in traditions because they have been handed down for many generations.

But after observation and analysis, when you find that anything agrees with reason and is conducive to the good and benefit of one and all, then accept it and live up to it.

—*Buddha*

Today, more than ever, we are deluged with hearsay. Radio, television, newspapers, and even the Internet traffic more in rumor and innuendo than in truth and ideas. So-and-so said that, so-and-so allegedly said or did such and such.

Daily, this is the kind of information we receive into our consciousness, along with a flood of advertisements.

And so I ask you, what is the point of all this promotion and gossip? Do we not have deeper, more pressing issues of our own and as a society to deal with, or are we so bored that we need this useless and trivial information to distract us?

Think what is happening to our minds. They are atrophying; they are slowly fading into habit and insensitivity. It is about time that we became more discerning, more critical minded and thoughtful, more intelligently independent and not simply dull receptors of this media-driven triviality and nonsense.

Guard well your spare moments. They are like uncut diamonds.
Discard them and their value will never be known.
Improve them and they will become the brightest
gems in a useful life.
—Ralph Waldo Emerson

How difficult to come by these days, these so-called spare moments. If you have lost yours, regain them. If you don't seem to have any, find some. Quiet time . . . times of contemplation . . . meditative moments give birth to the profound in us. Waste them and you waste the unknown seeds within you waiting to sprout. Waste them and you yourself begin to waste. In silence and solitude lies the soul of beauty.

*Look at everything as though you were seeing it
either for the first or last time.
Then your time on earth will be filled with glory.*
—Betty Smith

In the beginning, so shall it be in the end. But what about in-between? Can't we see gloriously in the days between the beginning and the end? Apparently not. We seem to build images of the things in our daily environment rather quickly. These images prevent us from actually seeing our wife, friend, couch, car, or closet. These images then become our reality, and this false reality bores and troubles us.

So, the trick is to let go of the images and truly see familiar things as if for the first time, every time.

Basically, all the world's mystical teachings come down to this very insight: to be able to see directly, without any barrier between the seer and the seen. This can't, despite what you may have heard, be taught. You simply have to try it; you simply have to allow it.

We know the truth, not only by the reason,
but also by the heart.
—Blaise Pascal

Reasoning can only take us so far. Eventually, we must listen to the answers of the heart. Today's bitterly divisive issues, such as capital punishment and abortion, are soundly reasoned on both sides. Each side is equally convinced of the virtue of its reasoning, so each side violently opposes the other side, and they go round and round. This vicious circle will continue until the heart decides. Let your heart be the final arbiter, and not merely a well-reasoned opinion, no matter how reasonable it may appear.

DAY 114 ◆ Spiritually Wise

Our scientific power has outrun our spiritual power.
We have guided missiles and misguided men.
—*Martin Luther King, Jr.*

Technology advances at a dizzying rate. Computers get more sophisticated daily. However, psychologically, we remain the same.

To what advantage are all these technological advances, these time-saving devices, if we know not what to do with our free time?

Idleness without wisdom breeds frustration. Frustration at its peak leads to violence. Our imperative, then, is to relieve the stress on our consciousness, to free our souls and become spiritually wise.

You may know the most complicated computer system, but if you know not peace of mind you know nothing.

*A beautiful thing never gives so much pain as
does failing to hear and see it.*
—Michelangelo

And so we have *David* and the Sistine Chapel, two of the world's greatest artistic triumphs, works of such grace and striking beauty, such wondrous and powerful dignity, that I'm certain none have passed by pained from having failed to look at them, for these works draw the heart and the eye, and require from each who comes into their presence some measure of appreciation, if not awe.

Perhaps the most pitiable and saddest failure for us as human beings is when we allow beauty to go unappreciated, when we pass it by with our hearts and senses closed.

To be vigilant and endeavor to appreciate the singing sparrow, the glowing yellow rose, the swaying eucalyptus, the poems of Whitman, the pictures of Monet, the music of Mozart, the smiling face, the pink sunset, the white half-moon, the sonorous waves, the cumulus clouds, and the simple sound of our own breathing is our duty and responsibility as people.

Happiness is not a goal, it is a by-product.
—*Eleanor Roosevelt*

When pressed, we say that the goal of life is happiness. But what is happiness? Can happiness be purchased at the local dealership? Should it be sought as the proverbial light at the end of the tunnel? Can or should it be sought? Can one person define happiness for another? How does one arrive at this state of being called happiness? Certainly these are important questions, questions that deserve our complete attention.

✦ Passion

One may have a blazing hearth in one's soul
and yet no one ever come to sit by it.
Passersby see only a wisp of smoke from the chimney
and continue on the way.
—Vincent van Gogh

Don't get discouraged if no one recognizes your burning desire for creation. Passion within, not that it be recognized, is the important thing. Recognition may come later. Keep the fire inside kindled.

Despite negativity, despite misunderstanding, despite uncertainty, despite despair, despite poverty and calumny, and even despite that annoying ringing in your ear, allow not the flaming truth of your heart to be stamped out.

Pursue your personal vision to the very end.

There are no days in life so memorable as those
which vibrated to some stroke of the imagination.
—*Ralph Waldo Emerson*

Imagination has given us the Taj Mahal, *Hamlet*, Beethoven's Fifth, the theory of relativity, the *Mona Lisa*, myths, computers, paper clips, and the list goes on and on. Certainly we are all the beneficiaries of those memorable days that spawned these imaginative leaps.

But we are all also the beneficiaries of those horrible imaginative leaps such as the gallows, the hydrogen bomb, television, crack cocaine, and more.

Blessed with the capacity to imagine, we imagine both good and evil.

Without a moral grounding the human imagination becomes a destructive force.

With a moral grounding the human imagination becomes a creative force.

DAY 119 ✦ Originality

*I had to create an equivalent for what I felt about what
I was looking at—not copy it.*
—Georgia O'Keeffe

This equivalent can still be seen and admired in her wonderful paintings, which display her unique vision.

Not to copy presents a difficult problem. American popular culture is by and large hackneyed and derivative. Simply watch television, listen to pop radio, shop in a mall, or go to a few movies, and this becomes readily apparent.

Originality is a rare and precious commodity that mostly goes unappreciated, or worse, is heaped with scorn. Most of us don't accept the responsibility of having our own thoughts and feelings about what we see. It is much safer and easier for us to borrow the thoughts and feelings of others, and so we live in an environment of staleness and monotonous repetition.

What is to be done, then? Try to think for yourself, and don't be disconcerted if your thoughts don't adhere to those around you. Be skeptical, and question everything until you come to a feeling about what you see, what you hear. Then your ears will be filled with your own music, and your eyes will be colored with your own vision.

I think I'm beginning to learn something about it.
—Pierre-Auguste Renoir
(at age seventy-eight, his last words about painting)

Learning should happily continue throughout life. To say "I know" and be done with it is to be among the living dead. How exciting life becomes when we are learning, creating, and engaging the new! Without learning our minds become weighty, dull, and sluggish. To keep an instrument sharp and in tune we must play it— play it well and often.

A mind is an incredibly complex instrument, the most complex instrument of all, with billions of synapses that start vigorously firing when we are learning. It is our instrument to waste or enhance. We can play it beautifully like a virtuoso, or we can make noise with it like an amateur. The choice is ours, now and to the end of our days.

DAY 121 ✦ Trial and Error

The things we have to learn before we can do them,
we learn by doing them.
—*Aristotle*

All day and all night long, your father could have explained to you how to ride a bike, but until you got on and pedaled, lost your balance and fell, got up and tried again, until finally you were joyously riding down the street, his explanations would not avail.

Try to build a toy by only using the instructions. Try to learn Microsoft Word by only reading the help files.

Attempting, learning, applying what you've learned, and trying again is how to master something

To be alive is to be learning.

*I put the relation of a fine teacher to a student
just below the relation of a mother to a son.*
—*Thomas Wolfe*

To be helpful without being overbearing, loving without being smothering, caring without being hindering, is to understand nurturing. Education requires that you walk beside your charge, not pull him from the front or push him from behind. Both student and teacher should put their best foot forward, and walk together along the road of development. Otherwise, a reciprocal resentment becomes part of the curriculum. The teacher resents having to reprimand or cajole the student, and the student resents being cajoled or reprimanded. It is vital, therefore, that the relationship be founded on trust and mutual respect, and that neither partner assume an attitude of superiority. Such is the way to make the journey along the path of education.

Derive happiness in oneself from a good day's work,
from illuminating the fog that surrounds us.
—Henri Matisse

Through practicing what is best in our natures, we find the light that illumines our days.

Perhaps a happy life consists simply of this: discovering and then practicing what is our natural talent.

Through neglecting what is best in our natures, we wander aimlessly in the fog.

Perhaps an unhappy life consists simply of this: avoiding and ignoring what is our natural talent.

DAY 124 ✦ Comprehension

Reading furnishes the mind only with materials of knowledge;
it is thinking that makes what we read ours.
—John Locke

We could memorize all these famous quotations, and repeat them ad infinitum, but this would in no way enhance our intelligence. Taking the time to examine each one, to understand what meaning they hold for us, and to learn from them, this will vitalize our minds.

Simply to repeat another's thought, concept, or idea, no matter how well it is expressed, no matter how original, displays a lazy mind. A parrot can do as much. Though they are beautiful in their way, we should aspire to be more than parrots. We must think!

DAY 125 ✦ Change

Though carefully wrapped, after a few days food begins to spoil. The pink rose blooms bright and fragrant, then its petals begin to shrivel and fall. Exposed to air, iron rusts. The sun itself is daily, wonderfully varied. After many millennia, a once lush rain forest becomes the Sahara desert. Caesar is no more, and life is ephemeral.

Everything changes, including us, in this mutable, beautiful universe, and this is its diligence.

DAY 126 ✦ The Present

The pleasure we derive from the representation of the present
is due not only to the beauty it can be clothed in,
but also to its essential quality of being the present.
—Charles Baudelaire

The present is the sculptor carving our past and forming our future. From its hands we are daily taking shape. Every blow from its hammer echoes into our future, and every tap of its chisel becomes a piece of our past. A work in progress, this hewing and shaping continues day and night. Such an indefatigable artist deserves our attention and respect. The range and scope and reach of its grasp leave us no choice but to live and love and learn under its tutelage. Indeed, it could be said without exaggeration that God is the present.

The Place of Knowledge

I had to set limits to knowledge
in order to make a place for faith.
—*Immanuel Kant*

Knowledge allows us to go grocery shopping, to build houses, to communicate, and to do invaluable things. Knowledge itself, though, is limited. Even the greatest genius can know only so much. So, it is significant for each of us to understand the proper place of knowledge in our lives. Knowing you were once happy will not lead you to present happiness. Spiritual knowledge is an oxymoron.

Faith and understanding, these are the concepts that apply in the realm of the spirit.

DAY 128 ✦ Obsession

Single-mindedness is all very well in cows or baboons;
in an animal claiming to belong to the same species as
Shakespeare it is simply disgraceful.
—Aldous Huxley

There's a difference between being purposeful and being obsessive. Having a purpose creates its own poise and equanimity. Having an obsession creates its own mania and stress. Obsession is purpose warped—purpose tormented and overwrought. We are the masters of our purposes, but the slaves of our obsessions. Being purposeful is to be motivated and principled. Being obsessive is to be compulsive and unscrupulous. We must be mindful that what starts out as a passionate purpose doesn't transform into a bewitching obsession. Allow room in your life for healthy, unrestrained enthusiasm but not for dominating, harassing fixations.

*The most immutable barrier in nature is between
one man's thoughts and another's.*
—William James

Upbringing and culture provide us with our opinions, tastes, and beliefs. One likes scallops, another hates scallops; one likes mysteries, another science fiction; one is a Hindu, another a Buddhist; one is a Republican, another a Democrat; one is pro-life, another pro-choice—and never the twain shall meet. Arbitrary and divisive, these opinions, tastes, and beliefs, when taken to the extreme, as they so often are, lead to violence and war.

Tolerance is not the answer. To simply tolerate someone means you loathe someone but won't act on that loathing. Understanding and compassion are required to overcome these nationalistic, religious, and cultural divisions.

Each of us must make the effort needed to free ourselves from our conditioning so we may live creatively and peaceably. Then we will see true diversity among neighbors, true expression without unthinking hatred based on unexamined bias.

DAY 130 ✦ You Are What You Eat

A man's character always takes its hue, more or less,
from the form and color of things about him.
—*Frederick Douglass*

Despite obtaining the choicest slice of beef, if you add it to rotten broth, it too will be spoiled.

Consider carefully whom it is you choose to spend your precious time with, and consider carefully where you choose to spend your precious time. Life requires diligence. Quality begets quality. Compassion nourishes compassion. Negativity suckles negativity. Choosing the proper atmosphere facilitates proper breathing. Friends are few but the corrupt are many.

See to it that you and yours grow in a properly nurturing garden.

Self-Possession

We are very much what others think of us.
The reception our observations meet with gives us courage
to proceed, or damps our efforts.
—William Hazlitt

Have you noticed that we act differently around different people?

Some think us humorous, so we act funny around them. Some think us serious, so we act serious around them. Some think us intelligent, so we act intelligent around them, while others think us immature, and so we act accordingly. This is why it can be very uncomfortable when we mix with a diverse group of friends and family. Being chameleons, we're not sure what color to wear in such a situation, so we simply blend into the bark.

But what about self-possession, that quiet confidence in ourselves that allows us to meet people and situations without acting, without acting as we think others expect us to act?

Play no more the role of clown, of scholar, of fool, of jock, of philosopher, of beauty, but be all these and more, only on your own terms.

All I really need to know about how to live and what to do
and how to be I learned in kindergarten. Remember the
Dick-and-Jane books and the first word you
learned—the biggest word of all—LOOK.
—Robert Fulghum

Yes, look! Look and see. Be aware of both the inward and
   outward movements in your life. Slow down, ease into your
   day, becoming thereby more observant, more relaxed.

Capable now of discovery, you will begin to discover,

Discover that strange, sculpturesque tree in your neighbor's
   yard;

Discover that hideous building downtown;

Discover that stunning mountain on your way to work;

Discover the unsightly trash strewn on the side of the road;

Discover the delicate hue of the sky;

Discover the anger of your neighbor;

Discover how truly angelic your wife is, or how handsome
   your husband is;

Discover the ravishing hues of the wildflowers in yonder field.

Yes, look, and you shall see, see the beauty and ugliness that
   everywhere surrounds you.

If a man does not keep pace with his companions,
perhaps it is because he hears a different drummer.
Let him step to the music which he hears,
however measured or far away.
—Henry David Thoreau

Allow for eccentricity in your life and in your neighbor's, for without it, life becomes monotonous. Music, painting, writing, science, all thrive on diversity and change. To fear and scorn those that are different is to stifle creativity. Too much clinging to tradition leaves us blind to the new. We become shocked and agitated when a Mozart plays, a Monet paints, an Einstein thinks, or a Joyce writes.

All that should give us joy provides us only with anxiety when we want only to dance to the Pied Piper's tune rather than to our own.

Life is not easy for any of us. But what of that?
We must have perseverance and above all confidence in ourselves.
We must believe that we are gifted for something
and that this thing must be attained.
—Marie Curie

To strive and strive again . . . to persevere in the face of calamity, to confront setbacks and move on, without diminishment of spirit, without feeling crushed and becoming heavy-eyed with despair, this is the true test of character. Make no mistake, life is a constant testing ground, a complete learning environment. Abrupt changes can and do occur without warning. Perseverance, confidence, and diligence, these things will guide us through life's shifting panorama.

Practice awareness, and that special gift, your unique ability to adapt to life's challenges, will appear to you like a lightning flash at midnight.

Well-timed silence hath more eloquence than speech.
—Martin Farquhar Tupper

How many times do you wish you could take back that ill-timed phrase, or that silly comment? Probably more times than you care to admit. For some unfathomable reason, we think that every word spoken to us requires ten words in response. Oftentimes, however, the appropriate response is a dignified silence. Not every question requires an answer or every statement another statement, as if we were all politicians with nothing better to do than to chatter. This also applies to the running dialogue in our heads. We need not be constantly talking within ourselves. After all, silence is the breeding ground of creation.

DAY 136 ✦ Nature

Everybody needs beauty as well as bread,
places to play in and pray in, where Nature may heal and cheer
and give strength to body and soul alike.
—*John Muir*

Too much time in the city, too many days of horns, helicopters, and sirens, and we're in need of nature's healing balm. A trip to a park, a hike in the wilderness, a sojourn on the beach, a climb up a mountain, will no doubt do to lift our spirits, to renew our energy, and to give us the strength and clarity of mind required for the days of horns, helicopters, and sirens to come.

Be sure to leave your radios and televisions at home on these outings, and be sure to pack your appreciation of beauty, the sound of birds, the touch of the wind, and the warmth of the sun.

There was never a great man
who had not a great mother.
—*Olive Schreiner*

O Mother, the quality time and loving effort you dedicated to me, I couldn't begin to repay.

When I was hungry, you fed me.

When I was thirsty, you quenched my thirst.

When I fell, you caught me.

When I laughed, you laughed with me.

When I cried, you comforted me.

When I first talked, you were there to listen—and you're still listening.

O Mother, the origin, the source, the creator, the bearer, the nurturer, the matriarch, and the generative loving goddess of all that is and will be, I love you.

What we observe is not nature itself,
but nature exposed to our method of questioning.
—Werner Karl Heisenberg

It's all in the mind's eye. Our perceptions color our world.

The chromatic sunset is blackened by our despair. The cloud-strewn night is afire with our joy. Harassed by our own minds, we miss much that is beautiful and calming, like the green grass in the wind, the serrated colors of dawn, the changing leaves in autumn, the explosion of flowers in spring, the white snowdrifts in winter, the pregnant fruit trees in summer, and many other wondrous sights.

Let us question our vision of the world, our worldview of fears and prejudices, and maybe with a little luck we may see things anew.

Everything has been figured out, except how to live.
—Jean-Paul Sartre

How to live cannot be figured out for us. Despite self-help books, philosophical treatises, religious pamphlets, and psychological texts, how to live remains a personal vision. One needs to forge one's life in the smithy of one's own soul.

By following, one is led, and the path leads not to happiness, but to another's ideas about happiness. Therefore, we must accept responsibility for how to live our own lives, and not expect other people, no matter how learned and well respected, to show us the way.

As individual and unique as our own features, as the era we live in, this life, our life, resists being charted, being clearly mapped out by anyone else, including parents and educators.

Though we might not understand it yet, only we know the way, and the way, our way, resides within us.

Anything will give up its secrets if you love it enough.
—George Washington Carver

Love is full of revelations . . . Love is many-eyed, and aware. Secrets locked deep in the tunnels of our hearts will open to us when in our hands are the keys of love. Open the chamber of your heart and your vision will follow. Then, without searching, love will discover for you the way; without your trying, love will provide the answer.

Without love, the sacred remains secret. Although it is within and around us, without love it remains hidden behind a veil of tears.

When one's expectations are reduced to zero,
one really appreciates everything one does have.
—*Stephen Hawking*

What are expectations? Using past knowledge in the present to project into the future. "I enjoyed my pasta last week, I think I'll have pasta for dinner tonight . . . last time I went to Mona's house I had a good time, so I hope to see her again this Saturday." These are expectations, and we all have them. The problem occurs when we think about the pasta dinner during breakfast or about Mona when we're at Jezebel's. By doing this, we fail to appreciate the cinnamon pancakes on our plate or Jezebel's auburn hair.

To be involved with and enjoy what one has now, one must be in the now.

Angels can fly because they take themselves lightly.
—*G. K. Chesterton*

With the weight of the world on our shoulders, getting off the ground becomes problematic. Our own minds have trouble soaring aloft because they are heavy laden with cares, anxieties, worries, remembrances, and deadlines of one sort or another. These things have a psychological weight, an abstract mass that smothers our imaginative capacity. Burdened so, we forget to lighten up, to let down our hair and go lightly through the days and nights— we forget about our wings, so our wings forget about us. Meanwhile, the angels of myth, like the birds in your neighborhood, fly on unencumbered.

*For one human being to love another, that is perhaps the most
difficult of our tasks; the ultimate, the last test and proof; the
work for which all other work is but preparation.*
—Rainer Maria Rilke

Relationships require attention, lest they become hedged about
with insecurities. Love, that singular flower, that life-changing experience, requires care and tending. You see, without our attention, love withers, becomes a memory that we cling to, and this
causes fear in our relationship, and fear leads to all manner of
troubles.

If love is ever evolving, ever new, then we must keep pace
with it, not stifle it because we're afraid of its protean character.
Hold not in your mind's eye yesterday's image of your loved one
and then compare it to today's reality of that person, for this will
only confuse and frustrate you. Instead, embrace openly what is
your loving relationship now.

When one door closes, another opens.
But we often look so regretfully upon the closed door
that we don't see the one which has opened for us.
—Alexander Graham Bell

Regret if you must, but don't waste too much energy on it. Say I wish I had or had not done this or that, and then get on with your life. To dwell on the past is to live in the house of the dead while the mansion of the living sits at your fingertips.

Quickly and honestly forgive yourself and those that may have wronged you, for therein lies the next open door—don't let that shut on you as well!

Yes, I do touch. I believe that everyone needs that.
—Diana, Princess of Wales

Touch is the most intimate of our senses. Touching, that palpable feeling we exchange through a handshake, a kiss, a massage, a squeeze of the shoulder, a pat on the back, or a hug can do more for those in distress than a thousand words. A sensitive caress can help alleviate the heaviest of burdens.

Children instinctively understand this, which is why they immediately look for the warmth and security of loving arms when they are upset.

For some strange reason, as grown-ups we lose that carefree willingness we had as children to show our feelings through touch—we become stingy when it comes to this sense.

Ordinary riches can be stolen, real riches cannot.
In your soul are infinitely precious things
that cannot be taken from you.
—Oscar Wilde

No one may trespass, no one may plunder your inner wealth without your consenting in some way. The inestimable things of the soul will not be corrupted or wagered away unless you yourself corrupt them or wager them away.

On the other hand, material possessions are there for the taking and made of flimsy stuff; therefore, utilize, but do not cling to them—understand that you are only borrowing them for a while, and that nothing material can ever be truly owned or entirely possessed.

Don't barter with your integrity, your dignity, or any of your spiritual treasures, and keep close to your heart the story of Faust.

The Best Advice

Nobody can give you wiser advice than yourself.
—*Cicero*

Since advice is based on experience and our own experiences are unique, then it follows that our most sage advice will come when we take counsel with ourselves. All of us at times seek the advice and counsel of friends and confidants, discuss with them our trials and tribulations and seek their guidance. Honestly, though, don't we ask for advice so as to confirm or get approval for whatever it is that we have decided? In the main, aren't we seeking high and low for a "yes"? This seems to be the case. Whether for good or ill we tend to act on our own counsel, despite the approval or the misgivings of others, and this is as it should be. After all, each of us reaps the ripe or bitter fruit of our own actions.

When we are chafed and fretted by small cares,
a look at the stars will show us the littleness
of our own interests.
—Maria Mitchell

Small cares can present large problems, for they tend to obscure clear thinking. A look to the heavens, to the endless expanse of starry space at night, does plenty to dissolve the petty problems accumulated during the day.

To gaze at the stars and see our own life reflected therein; to be touched by light that has traveled innumerable miles, is to be both calmed and awed by the miracle of it all, the incredible improbability that the universe is, and we are of it.

*A person's mind stretched to a new idea never goes back
to its original dimensions.*
—Oliver Wendell Holmes

The thrill of insight is certainly one of the wonderful things in life. Once our minds make a new synaptic connection the insight remains, like a precious heirloom, always ours. How easily and quickly we now give the answer to "What is two times two?" when once upon a time we struggled with this simple multiplication. Similarly, how impossibly difficult is it for some of us to remember how to find the hypotenuse of a triangle because we never quite liked or "got" geometry.

While certainly liberating, a new idea can also be life changing. Witness the mental revolution brought on by Einstein's theory of relativity. The human mind stretched to reach the dimensions of this theory and has never gone back.

Liberating and life-changing, a new idea must have an open mind to grow within. Our duty to our fellowmen and ourselves is to possess and nourish that open mind.

DAY 150 ✦ Hatred

I will permit no man to narrow and degrade my
soul by making me hate him.
—Booker T. Washington

Hatred is insidious. Like a plague it can seep into our souls and hideously affect all our innate beauty and goodness. Long and degraded is a life filled with bitterness and hatred. We must remain ever vigilant against this destructive disease—not allowing it to spread within unawares. To seek a cure, we first have to acknowledge the proclivity to hate in our daily lives. Only when we acknowledge it and see its ill effects will we be able to find the proper remedy.

*For the sin they do by two and two they
must pay for one by one.*
—*Rudyard Kipling*

Many persons form a group, yet ten thousand can still be reduced to their individual numbers; therefore, the wicked will find no refuge in numbers and no excuse in the many.

If you are in the play, it makes little difference whether your lines were few or many, but only that you played a part. Think not that because your part was small, your significance was little and your responsibility none. Without its full cast of characters, a company cannot perform the show. From the silent extra sitting in a corner for effect to the vociferous leading man and woman, all play their roles in the tragedy, and each alone must answer for the performance after the curtain falls.

*One of the symptoms of an approaching nervous breakdown
is the belief that one's work is terribly important.*
—Bertrand Russell

Stress and anxiety occur when we take our occupations and ourselves too seriously. After all, only a few perform open-heart surgery, while the rest of us are selling something or making something to be sold.

Is it terribly important that you sold only ten mouse pads, three insurance policies, or five cars; or that you didn't make twenty-two toothbrushes, eight hundred paper clips, or fifteen widgets? Should not your peace of mind come before your piece of the pie? We need perspective. We need to put what we do in its proper context.

We need to see the entire screen of life and not just the prime-time show that we think of as our lives.

Technology

*It has become appallingly obvious that our technology
has exceeded our humanity.*
—Albert Einstein

Technology without compassion breeds destruction. Consider the manpower, the effort, and the genius that went into making the first nuclear weapon. And for what, to reduce other human beings to ashes? Now, many different countries are equipped with weapons of mass destruction. This means, throughout the world, supposedly intelligent men such as physicists and engineers have expended their energy, spent their time on death and destruction.

Is this what is meant by progress? Are we really intelligent beings? Emotionally, it seems, we still live in caves and wield clubs, despite our computers, jet planes, and microwaves.

Every animal knows more than you do.
—Native American proverb

What do the eagle, the deer, and the alligator know that we don't know? The eagle knows the blue sky, the freedom of flight; the deer knows the forest, the abundance of foliage; and the alligator knows the lake, the wealth of the water. But more than just knowing their worlds they are at home in them, comfortable in their environments, while we seem uncomfortable in this world, not quite at our ease.

Beauty as we feel it is something indescribable,
what it is or what it means can never be said.
—*George Santayana*

I wish I could say more about beauty than a walnut tree in bloom, the Pacific Ocean at noon, or a leopard on a termite mound. I long to say other things besides the sunset, the half-moon rising, and the first star at twilight, but I know not what. Perhaps it's simpler just to say, *Irises*, "Ode to Joy," and *The Dhammapada*, or even mothers, fathers, sons, and daughters . . .

DAY 156 ✦ Hunger

There are people in the world so hungry that God cannot appear to them except in the form of bread.
—Mahatma Gandhi

When younger, I never understood saying grace before a meal. To me, it was simply another needless delay. Now, I clearly see what a privilege, a blessing it is to have three meals a day. Let us not be ungrateful but thankful, thankful that we don't go hungry and that the earth has seen fit to provide us with our daily bread. It is time to praise the earth and it splendorous bounty, and time to curse ourselves and be ashamed for the hunger that exists in this world in an age of such abundance.

And whosoever will, let him take the water of life freely.
—Revelation 22:17

All those days of rain—
The rain-soaked evenings, the dew-drenched mornings—
Created this riot of verdure,
This exploding rainbow of color.
How else to celebrate it but by composing a song?
After all, her abundant, wild hair so suddenly loosed
Is like so many musical notes, so many various
Phrases harmonizing on the earth.

Look at the flowers, full and flowing strings;
Look at the trees, a sweet-sounding wind section;
And the grass, a delicately evocative concertina;
Yes, all those days of rain—
The rain-soaked evenings and the dew-drenched mornings—
Composed this lush symphony, this chromatic concert, all this
thriving life.

*The avaricious man is like the barren sandy ground
of the desert which sucks in all the rain and dew with
greediness, but yields no fruitful herbs
or plants for the benefit of others.*
—Zeno

GREED IN TWO ACTS

Act I

Evolution abhors avarice, and the greedier the species, the quicker its demise. Along with earning you the wrath and disdain of your fellow creatures, avarice takes a tremendous amount of time and energy, leaving little time for anything but its own perpetuation. Caught in the vicious cycle of coveting, acquiring, and hoarding, the greedy not only deprive others of basic needs but also deprive themselves of even the most common satisfactions. Too busy stuffing his face, a glutton never enjoys a meal.

Act II

Despite its many forms—some covet pleasure, things, feelings, fame—greed begins and endures because of an insatiable inner dissatisfaction. People afflicted try through acquisitiveness to quell their horribly grating discontent, but are unsuccessful, for the simple reason that no amount of acquisitions can slake the intemperate thirst of spiritual disquiet. To satisfy such thirst, one must first free oneself form the outward manifestations of the problem, the greediness, and then one can engage the source, the discontent.

✦ Self-Satisfaction

To love oneself is the beginning of a lifelong romance.
—*Oscar Wilde*

Appreciating our own company, being content while alone with ourselves, rather than restless and uneasy, is a tremendously consequential achievement. Imagine spending an entire day alone, without tormenting yourself—imagine walking alone in a forest without anxiety or discomfort, feeling carefree and unhurried. This peacefulness within, this ability to be alone without being lonely, requires the equanimity that comes from "knowing thyself." Without it we are doomed to recurring bouts of disquiet.

DAY 160 ✦ What Is Love?

Everyone admits that love is wonderful and necessary,
yet no one agrees on just what it is.
—Diane Ackerman

Love is a fountain, a flower, and a friend;
Love is a feeling, an understanding, and a revelation;
Love is compassion, beauty, and truth;
Love is tolerant, patient, and giving;
Love is freedom, redemption, and completion;
Love is natural, sweet, and kind;
Love is gentle, peaceful, and graceful;
Love is passionate, affectionate, and elegant;
Love is saintly, princely, and healthy;
Love is intoxicating, yes, a thing undefined yet divine!

I have spread my dreams under your feet;
Tread softly because you tread on my dreams.
—William Butler Yeats

Be sensitive to those with whom you are most intimate. A great confidence has been exchanged between each of you, a delicate trust upon which rests the foundation of society. If you can't even love your spouse, sister, brother, mother, father, or friend, how can you then expect to love your neighbor?

Can we honestly envision our children having healthy, loving adult relationships when they grow up observing antagonism, enmity, within their own families? Surely, we ourselves must learn the art of relationship before we look for any significant changes in generations to come.

Forgive those close to you for knowing you so well. Set aside your fears and insecurities and relate directly to those you love without judgment, but with understanding and sensitivity. After all, if you can't relate to them, whom can you relate to?

The whole problem with the world is that fools and fanatics
are always so certain of themselves,
but wiser people so full of doubts.
—*Bertrand Russell*

A healthy disquiet, a rumbling within, perhaps heralds the change you've been awaiting, so do not escape from, but embrace the disturbance. To doubt, to ponder and to question, this is the essence of self-discovery, the very root of growth.

Those that proclaim they know and that's that are but displaying their complete immersion in their conditioning. When we begin to seriously question, then we begin to see that all we were taught might not be golden; indeed, it may be the reason for our unhappiness and our inability to overcome sorrow.

Why is it so painful to watch a person sink? Because there is something unnatural in it, for nature demands personal progress, evolution, and every backward step means wasted energy.
—*August Strindberg*

We may feel at times like we're falling headlong down the stairs of our own unraveling, when in fact we are falling forward into greater progress. Though we often don't see it while the skein of our lives is spinning out of control, we yet may realize in the aftermath that we've gained in stature, and that what once seemed like a catastrophic period in life was really only a difficult part of personal evolution.

Growing pains are part of growth. What is painful and disturbing to watch is a person who fails to accept this and loses faith, who sinks only to remain sunk.

The most beautiful thing we can experience is the mysterious.
It is the source of all true art and science.
—Albert Einstein

A blade of grass, an ant on a leaf, the leaf itself, and the tree that spawned it provoke wonder because of their inherent mystery. Verily, life itself is mysterious, not only mysterious but a complete mystery.

How incalculable the sun, planets, moon and stars;
How unfathomable the fish and mammals in the sea;
How intricate the flowers; how mystifying the atmosphere;
How cryptic our ancestors; how inscrutable the dinosaurs;
How inexplicable the beginning; how impenetrable the end;
How marvelous and intriguing that cat on your doorstep,
The glass in your hand and the face reflected therein.

*Every child is an artist. The problem is how
to remain an artist once he grows up.*
—*Pablo Picasso*

Both child and artist see the world directly and with ever-fresh eyes. This creative seeing, while natural for the child, requires much effort for the artist. Mostly, only the artist attempts the struggle and striving required to possess this childlike vision. Every adult should be an artist. Every adult should reacquire the dynamic vision he or she had as a child.

An artistic journey is best begun by unfamiliarizing ourselves with the familiar, by seeing the uncommon in the common, and the new in the so-called old. Thus, we may eventually see the wonder in all that is wonderful.

Call on God, but row away from the rocks.
—*Indian proverb*

Life will assist you in your heartfelt endeavors but will not act for you. However much you pray, however much you beg and cry out, life will not do for you if you won't do for yourself. Despite the painter's being supplied with easel, canvas, brush, and paints, unless he picks up the brush and employs the imagination and talent bequeathed to him, he has but a potential masterpiece.

The Creator has not given you a longing to do
that which you have no ability to do.
—Orison S. Marden

Deep down, on a moonless night or a cloudy afternoon, on a Sunday morning or on a Tuesday at midnight, in the grocery store or in your bed, while driving on the freeway or taking a walk, do you long to create, do you have a searing aspiration to be an artist? Then deny yourself no longer.

The anguish of not following your bliss debilitates. Acknowledge your longing—it is not too late. Find the space and time to develop your creative abilities. Life is short, but a truly creative life recognizes no time at all. Begin!

*If some great catastrophe is not announced every morning, we feel
a certain void. Nothing in the paper today, we sigh.*
—Paul Valéry

Filled with an ever-growing ennui, an ever-increasing boredom,
we receive a sick thrill, a slight quickening of the heart upon
hearing of some great tragedy. Each night we turn on the evening
news to be mesmerized by the latest horrific crimes, the most
recent scandals, and all the freshest gossip.

Indeed, what is even worse than this vicarious thrill is the fact
that we are so inundated with tragedies that we have become
nearly immune to them, and only the grandest catastrophes now
move us. And so the world begins to fill with oceans of unshed
tears.

Neither fire nor wind, birth nor death,
can erase our good deeds.
—Buddha

Good deeds carry within them their own momentum, their own positive life force that keeps them acting on earth into perpetuity. The immediate effects of a good deed may or may not be apparent, but it is impossible to trace the residual effects of a good deed, as goodness expands exponentially. And to those who performed the good deed, the credit remanded to them remains imperishable, a part of their consciousness forever.

The man who goes alone can start today, but he who travels
with another must wait till that other is ready.
—Henry David Thoreau

Man cannot exist in isolation, but all the same, each man is an island, and from the beginning, into the middle, and at the end, he goes it alone.

To discover truths about oneself one must travel the dark and winding road within. None can go the journey with us. Though some kindly soul may provide us with a flashlight, it is up to us to turn it on, and use it to illuminate our way.

Wait for no one, your time is not theirs, but begin soon, really soon, even if by moonlight.

Therefore we do not lose heart.
Even though our outward man is perishing,
yet the inward man is being renewed day by day.
—*2 Corinthians 4:16*

Woe to you who spent your entire life concerned with your appearance: That accident of birth, your beauty, will soon be the bane of your days. Old age requires more than merely the memories of a now-faded beauty for it to be golden. Nothing is more gorgeous in a human being than that person's unseen beauty, the kind that may take nearly a lifetime to cultivate, and nothing sadder than a person who doesn't wear his or her age well.

The young at heart are at home in every generation.

DAY 172 ◆ Appearance

*When I see a bird that walks like a duck and swims like a duck
and quacks like a duck, I call that bird a duck.*
—*Richard C. Cushing*

Unfortunately, appearances, at times, do matter. I know, you shouldn't judge a book by its cover, but if you're a white guy with a shaved head and a swastika tattooed on your arm, I won't be coming to your birthday party despite what a great guy your friends say you are. One must practice discernment, because sometimes the clothes do make the man, and the outside does reflect the inside.

A duck will never be a swan, will never swim with that ebullient grace.

Common sense is not so common.
— *Voltaire*

When pressured, our best ally, our common sense, gets waylaid.

In a hurry to get home, we decide to take a shortcut through the dark and seemingly deserted city park.

Look out! There in the bushes . . . too late, we just got mugged and nearly lost our life. Where was our common sense when we decided on the shortcut? In our haste we cleverly pushed it aside.

Oftentimes the simple answer is the most sensible, but we're suspicious of what's simple and we overthink ourselves into difficulties. "It couldn't be that easy," we say to ourselves and before we know it, we're in a sophisticated mess.

Haven't you yet noticed that your soundest judgments and your most prudent assessments have often been generated not by intellectualizing but by good old common sense?

Today was good. Today was fun.
Tomorrow is another one.
—Doctor Seuss

Search where you will, but I doubt you'll find a simpler, more life-affirming mantra than this one by the creator of *The Cat in the Hat*, Theodor Geisel.

Honestly, when did you last feel this way? If it's been too long ago, then it is time to make the appropriate changes. Let no more the ashes of despair settle on your days. Start cleaning your spirit today, because today can be good. Today can be fun.

Remember, it's up to each of us to make what we will of our own days, and we can build them well or build them ill, but they will be done, and tomorrow is another one.

*Anger will never disappear so long as thoughts of resentment
are cherished in the mind. Anger will disappear just
as soon as thoughts of resentment are forgotten.*
—*Buddha*

On rocks, resentment, wine, and wrath:

Cling not to the stubborn rock of your resentment, but let it roll away, lest you crush yourself through hating your enemy.

Hold rancor no longer but let it seep from your mind like the dew from the rock of ages.

Resentment is the hangover of anger and one sip from its bottle, and you will be drunk again with rage.

A sober-minded man intoxicates himself only on the sweet, delicate, and heady wine of sensitivity, while letting all the grapes of wrath rot in the vineyards of their own distaste.

They defend their errors as if
they were defending their inheritance.
—Edmund Burke

Own it and move on. We get so attached to our beliefs that we grow foolhardy and obstinate.

Despite clear and convincing evidence to the contrary, we sometimes cling tooth and nail to our errors if they are backed up by long-held beliefs. So attached do we become to our beliefs that we would sacrifice our betterment rather than admit we held an erroneous view.

What happened to humility and a willingness to grow? Why can't we see the dignity and courage involved in admitting we were mistaken, misguided, or simply wrong? Why can't we see that such admissions come complete with the prestigious mantle of self-improvement?

✦ Attitude Adjustment

It is not fitting, when one is in God's service,
to have a gloomy face or a chilling look.
—*Saint Francis of Assisi*

Why so sullen and gloomy, Jim? Why so glum and forbidding, Jane? Smile, for life is short. Take that dour look off your face: Unfurrow your brow, unpurse your lips, and remove that obstinate stare from your eyes.

Surely a stern attitude is self-perpetuating. An icy glare is returned in kind, as cheerless looks are contagious. Give it up, even if by force of will. Change your physiognomy and it will change you. Smile, for life is short.

DAY 178 ✦ Exuberance

Exuberance is beauty.
—William Blake

Nature is nothing if not exuberant:

The richness of spring running riot with wildflowers across the Rhode Island countryside;

The abundance of summer corn streaming behind an Amish barn;

The hoard of prismatic leaves whispering earthward on a breezy autumn morning in Vermont;

The copious snowflakes bleaching the Blue Mountains of Virginia on a winter's evening.

Match this natural exuberance and we too shall know beauty.

*I am doing a great work and I cannot come down. Why should
the work stop while I leave it and come down to you?*
—*source unknown*

"Michelangelo, come down off that scaffolding and let's go have
a drink."

I bet Michelangelo would have answered with this quote if
anyone had been blind enough to make such a silly request
of him.

Any work of magnitude requires integrity of purpose and an
intractable dedication. The distractions are legion, but the work
is singular. Despite intrusive invitations and envious cajoling, the
show must go on.

Why should the work stop? Why should you leave it when
your very blood desires its fruition? Many are called, but only a
few come, so don't let the many that didn't answer their calling
call you away from your passion. You owe it to the rest of us
and to posterity to finish your ceiling.

I am returning this otherwise good typing paper to you
because someone has printed gibberish all over it
and put your name at the top.
—*English professor, Ohio University*

Better not to make an effort than to make a half-hearted one. Better to refuse outright an assignment than to accept it reluctantly and perform it inadequately. It's a misguided sense of duty that finds us engaged in things we otherwise don't want or have to do. This kind of acquiescence is responsibility turned inside out, because the result of such accommodation usually translates into acquitting ourselves poorly, irresponsibly.

Of course, we oftentimes find ourselves in the position of having to do things we'd rather not do, but the task becomes only more wearisome and annoying when we do it begrudgingly and inattentively. Why not, then, perform with equal parts equanimity and self-respect those unwelcome duties that invariably confront us?

Eccentricity is not, as dull people would have us believe, a form of madness. It is often a kind of innocent pride, and the man of genius and the aristocrat are frequently regarded as eccentrics because the genius and aristocrat are entirely unafraid of and uninfluenced by the opinions and vagaries of the crowd.
—*Dame Edith Sitwell*

Opinion holds great sway in our lives. Simply observe your own mad attempts to remain fashionable. Amid the changing fashions in cars and clothes, and so forth, keeping up with the Joneses assumes unnatural proportions.

Why is being different in a supposedly free society such an anathema? Even the kids who get tattoos or nose rings aren't being different; they're merely trying to conform to their particular group. Though their clothes are clean and well suited to them, we still tend to look mockingly at the elderly who at long last have disdained to buy into fads, we having failed to realize in our latest designer jeans that true style is never antiquated.

Style is not a fad but a state of being. A stylish woman will wear her grandmother's dress with grace, whereas a woman who runs with the fashions may well look slovenly in a state-of-the-art Gucci outfit. So before we look askance at a so-called eccentric, we might first take a long hard look in the mirror.

Piglet sauntered up to Pooh from behind. "Pooh!" he whispered.
"Yes, Piglet?" "Nothing," said Piglet, taking Pooh's paw,
"I just wanted to be sure of you."
—A. A. Milne

Are you still there? It's been 182 days, and we've covered a lot of spiritual ground, been given a lot to digest. So I just wanted to be sure of you, for as Piglet is nothing without Pooh, so a writer is nothing without readers, especially attentive ones.

Together we will continue on the daily, uncertain road of discovery, and we may just find ourselves a little better at living for taking this trip.

Illusions commend themselves to us because they save us pain and
allow us to enjoy pleasure instead. We must therefore accept
it without complaint when they sometimes collide with a
bit of reality against which they are dashed to pieces.
—*Sigmund Freud*

If we insist on harboring illusions we must accept how easily and severely they can be shattered. The longer and more persistent our self-deception, the more devastated we feel when reality comes home to roost. In a divorce, the party most painfully affected by the proceedings is the one who insistently refused to acknowledge the problems in the relationship.

You see, the pleasures we enjoy from illusions are but debts we incur that must eventually be paid in pain. Relentless reality will out. Consequently, try not to savor your illusions, but see them for what they are, appealing escape mechanisms, and when the veil of one of your comforting illusions is lifted, try not to act so surprised.

A room without books
is like a body without a soul.
—*Cicero*

Fill your body with the soul of good books. Read not only for pleasure, but also for understanding. Engage the book, don't simply sail through it like it's a calm, sunny day's diversion—as if you could learn something simply being along for the ride, a passive passenger in a deck chair—but take it on as if you were the skipper navigating through a treacherous storm.

A book is nothing to you if it is not a violent storm, a hurricane provoking your mind into action. In other words, read actively.

A man's very highest moment is, I have no doubt at all,
when he kneels in the dust, and beats his breast,
and tells all the sins of his life.
—Oscar Wilde

When life humbles us to such a point of despair that we feel
broken and worthless, there is nothing left but to get it all out,
to face squarely the shortcomings that led us to such a state. This
is not to say that should we find ourselves in this abandoned
condition we should blame ourselves, only that we confess, honestly acknowledge our role, which in itself is a cleansing act of
contrition. It would appear that despondency of this nature should
be one of our lowest moments and not one of our highest, but
as owning up takes great courage and bespeaks of a profound
change of attitude, it becomes, if we allow it, a watershed moment
of great importance.

*Divide each difficulty into as many parts as is
feasible and necessary to resolve it.*
—René Descartes

Simplifying a problem by breaking it down into its component parts is an important skill, a skill worth mastering due to its breadth of application. Not only is this skill of practical value in the common affairs of science and business, but also in dealing with the difficulties of relationships.

Instead of considering the complexities of a long-standing relationship too difficult to master and leaving it at that, perhaps if we divided the problem we may be having into parts, we could conquer it and thus reenter the world of healthy relationships.

Presumably, somewhere along the line in the puzzle of our now troubled relationship, all the pieces fit; otherwise, how could we have come this far? Although through the auspices of time and change the pieces may presently be scrambled, they are essentially the same and will bear redesigning—if, that is, we have the desire to discover which pieces are essential, and the patience to take them one piece at a time.

The tighter you squeeze, the less you have.
—Zen saying

Hold tight to your breast that luscious mango and you will end with a dry, wrinkled fruit. Cling to your fancy new car and its first scratch will see you beside yourself with fury. Rely on another for emotional support and the minute things become uncertain, and they are unavailable, you will tremble with despair. Attach your mind narrowly to beliefs and watch as senility rears its ugly head. Yet, unhinge your mind from the jamb of attachment and see the beauty of evanescence—this world.

Self-Transformation

*We are celebrating the feast of the Eternal Birth which
God the Father has borne and never ceases to bear in
all eternity. . . . But if it takes not place in me, what avails it?
Everything lies in this, that it should take place in me.*
—Meister Eckehart

The "eternal present" . . . "the holy now" . . . "all is one" and all
the rest of spirituality is reduced to mystical psychobabble lest
we ourselves feel in our own hearts the truth.

What avails proclaiming the brotherhood of man when we
mistreat our brothers?

What avails it to say "love thy neighbor" when we talk ill of
our neighbor?

What avails the oneness of all when we live divisively?

Nothing avails and the world spins heedlessly and we walk
from pleasure to pain and back again, unless we transform ourselves, unless our own hearts blossom with insight.

Fear has many eyes and can see things underground.
—Miguel de Cervantes

Not many things in this world are as bad as we are afraid they'll be.

Fear itself creates the Medusa's head of our fears, and since we will only look askance at it, we see its serpents everywhere. By not responding adequately to the issue of fear, we are prone to many fears: fear of flying, fear of water, fear of intimacy, fear of heights, fear of crowds, fear of small spaces, and more.

How do we respond adequately, and whence does fear and all its many faces come? Of what, finally, are we most afraid? Death—the inevitability of dying and its handmaiden, the unknown—it is of this that we are most afraid. Our own mortality scares the hell out of us. The insecurity of being always at death's door, and not knowing what's on the other side, creates the many-eyed monster of fear.

As to a method for putting an end to a fear of the end, I'm afraid I don't know one. Maybe it's love, maybe laughter, maybe truth, maybe religion, maybe philosophy, or maybe it's one of those things that will take a lifetime to understand.

Faith has to do with things that are not seen,
and hope with things that are not in hand.
—*Saint Thomas Aquinas*

One may hope to win the lottery, but one has faith in the
spirit.

Hope may spring eternal, but faith springs internal.

Hope has to do with desire, and faith with trust.

Hope clings, while faith lets go.

Hope leads to despair, faith never.

Faith may, as it were, remove mountains, hope never.

You may hope against hope that things will get better, but
faith, especially in yourself, will see that it is so.

Faith comprehends without seeing, hope imagines without
comprehending.

Hope is hedged about by doubt, faith never.

Faith is like the salt in the ocean; you may not see it, yet you
know that it's there.

Teach thy tongue to say I do not know
and thou shalt progress.
—*Maimonides*

Confess your spiritual ignorance, be honest about not knowing, and in that way you may begin to find out. It takes tremendous humility to begin the inward journey. Not only humility, but also a clarity of mind. One must start the journey with a clean slate. To blaze a new trail, one must let go of all preconceived notions about where the journey may lead. Unencumbered by the pride of knowledge, we humbly approach the mysteries of the soul.

DAY 192 ◆ Feeding the Mind

I grow old learning something new every day.
—*Solon*

Remain physically inert and your bones atrophy; remain mentally inert and your mind atrophies. The mind needs as much nourishment as the body. New and interesting things must be fed to it, else it deteriorates from malnourishment. Too many people stop learning, stop mentally ruminating the moment they finish school. They become mentally complacent and set their minds into a rigid routine—indulge in the same mental repast day in and day out.

However, to treat your mind like a fast-food depot will only find you one day "old and gray and full of sleep and nodding by the fire . . ." with nothing of creative value to show that you have lived and learned.

One must cultivate the mind; feed and nurture, water and prune it, lest it wither from want of care.

DAY 193 ✦ Perseverance

*Our greatest glory is not in never failing but
in rising up every time we fail.*
—Ralph Waldo Emerson

At times we must labor valiantly to get up off the canvas after one of life's severer thrashings. Yet arise we do. We may have to scratch and kick our way up, but up we get. Amazing, the tragedies that occur to some of us and yet still we persist; still we engage in life's daily activities: We wake, love, and live on into the night "of cloudless climes and starry skies."

Why? Because Life Is Beautiful.

The images of the unconscious place a great responsibility upon a man. Failure to understand them, or a shirking of ethical responsibility, deprives him of his wholeness and imposes a painful fragmentariness on his life.
—Carl Jung

So much that is baffling goes on under the surface. Millennia of images along with our own bizarre inner slide show are meant to be stored in your unconscious. And we're supposed to make heads or tails of it? I for one am glad he threw in that part about "ethical responsibility." This certainly makes things easier. If we can't through our dreams and subtle acts decipher the *Rocky Horror Picture Show* that is our unconscious, we can at the very least not shirk our ethical responsibility.

By the way, what is your ethical responsibility? Do you know? Have you ever asked yourself? Considering the choices and the fact that we would all rather be whole than fragmentary, why not give this question some thought?

Children today are tyrants.
They contradict their parents, gobble their food,
and tyrannize their teachers.
—Socrates

Some things never change, save that now we can unhappily add to this list that children kill their classmates, shoot them in cold blood. We are a long, sad way from just contradicting parents and gobbling food. Let us disarm our children both physically and psychologically; let us teach them that violence begets violence and nothing ever gets resolved in this manner. Perhaps we should reconsider the amount of violence we expose them to at such early ages. Perhaps television violence does rerun as violence in the streets, actual violence with real children being killed. Mostly, though, we should talk with our children, be aware of their emerging feelings and difficulties, and help them as only parents can, by listening and by truly caring.

*In all things it is a good idea to hang a question mark now
and then on the things we have taken for granted.*
—*Bertrand Russell*

Car? Appliances? Clothes? House? Money? Pets? Health? Food?
Friends? Lovers? Family? Nature? Living? God?

Give sorrow words.
— William Shakespeare

A yawning abyss, a gaping wound that swallows and at the same time marks the time—this is sorrow. Express your sorrow. Don't be ashamed of it. Every person who has lived on this earth has experienced sorrow. No longer deny suffering.

Take off that phony mask and come to the ballroom exposed. Face sorrow and it will face you and only then may you study it properly—only then may you come to understand it, and yourself . . . only then may you sing and dance.

Not the fruit of experience but experience itself, is the end.
—Walter Pater

Once again, we see that life is in the living and not in the getting. We want the fruit all ripe and ready but we don't want to spend time tending the tree. Foreplay be damned, we want the harvest. Results now! This is the new-age mantra. Give me liberty or give me a new car; either way, I don't want to work too hard.

In our haste, we've forgotten what it means to live like artisans, skilled craftsmen for whom the creating is the important thing. Being results-oriented, we forget about quality, and quality suffers. But if we consider how truly tasty homegrown fruit is, how delectable the apple from a tree that was nurtured with care and attention, then we may well see the virtue of patience, the delight in growing for its own sake.

*It is the common wonder of all men, how among
so many million faces, there should be none alike.*
—*Sir Thomas Browne*

Make that so many billion faces. Imagine, using the same basic features as a template, the incredible inventiveness required to produce this startling diversity. Maybe your face won't launch a thousand ships, but it's uniquely yours all the same. Your face is not just any face, but your own face.

Seeing the diversity of hues and features that make a face, why not celebrate this variety instead of denigrate it? Differences should be the delight of life and not its bane. You may well resemble your mother, but what of it? Someone else resembles his or her mother, and so it goes. All of us were born of mothers and with that singular face most suited to our lives, so wear it well.

No duty is more urgent than that of returning thanks.
—Saint Ambrose

Life requires our adoration and appreciation. When we become selfish and complacent, and take life's abundance for granted, it inevitably provides us with a harsh and unforgettable wake-up call. This call is part of the price exacted by life, to remind us that we were born free, and that to maintain this freedom requires a certain quality of awareness, as well as a certain amount of gratefulness and praise.

Many are the nights of anguish and travail when we've become so self-centered as to lose touch with our spirit. To treat the gift of life as anything other than a sacred gift is to be mercenary, and to invite the wrath of the gods.

Difficulties are things that show a person what he is.
—Epictetus

In the midst of travail, amid the confusion of desperate circumstances, we find out the stuff from which we are made. If we are
noble, our nobility will shine; if compassionate, our compassion
will shine; if petty and vindictive, our pettiness and vindictiveness
will shine. It is one thing to be noble and compassionate on the
couch watching the six o'clock news, and quite another to be
noble and compassionate while engaged in the difficulties of
daily relationship.

To forget one's purpose is the commonest form of stupidity.
—*Friedrich Nietzsche*

Family, friends, work, lovers, all can divert us from our chartered course. We often get sidetracked and end up docked in an unfamiliar port, often led there by the good intentions of our intimates.

The important point is not that we have gotten sidetracked, but that we get back on course, get back to our purpose. Certainly, you first need to know your purpose, to find your meaning, before you can be led astray, be carried away in a delirium of fortuitous circumstance.

If we live too long in distraction, it becomes habitual and we lose, to our detriment, our focus and driving passion.

DAY 203 ✦ Promises

Those that are the most slow in making a promise
are the most faithful in the performance of it.
—Jean-Jacques Rousseau

Indeed, promises made rashly, despite the best intentions, tend not to be fulfilled or are fulfilled inadequately, and someone's feelings get hurt. Though some of us find this hard to understand, the word *no* is its own kind of promise, and it isn't always a negative. At times, to say no is a promise to yourself, the promise to be true to your heart.

For the most part, we say yes so readily because we are eager to please others, but to please another while displeasing yourself will eventually encourage you to begrudge the other and chide yourself.

We are responsible for what we are, and whatever we wish ourselves to be, we have the power to make ourselves. If what we are now has been the result of our own past actions, it certainly follows that whatever we wish to be in future can be produced by our present actions; so we have to know how to act.
—*Swami Vivekenanda*

And we have to act now or forever dread our future. Who wants to be in the same predicament, with the same fears and anxieties, the same thought patterns, ten years from now? Shall we not, instead, break the monotonous cycle now; shall we not utilize our present power to change our future circumstances?

The ball has been served. It's now on your side of the court. Return it how and where you will, but return it.

I have known it for a long time but I have only just experienced it.
Now I know it not only with my intellect, but with my eyes,
with my heart, with my stomach.
—*Hermann Hesse*

Explain to your friend the wonders of the Grand Canyon and he may say, "Yes, I know . . . I've heard it's amazing," or "I've seen photographs," but until he's been there and seen with his own eyes the vast splendor of it, felt in his very entrails the immensity of it, the magnificence, he doesn't know it.

So it is with inner experience; nothing can substitute for it.

One must first have had to shed tears to know that they taste salty and bittersweet.

DAY 206 ✦ Avoidance

Ye shall know the truth, and the truth shall make you mad.
—Aldous Huxley

At times the truth angers and frustrates us. Nonetheless, for all that, it is still the truth. We must not avoid the truth because of our fear of pain, for in such avoidance lies even greater anguish. If the truth angers, then be angry without pretense; if the truth disgusts, then be disgusted without pretense. This is the way to understanding: facing what is directly, facing what is without falsification.

Our grand business is not to see what lies dimly at a distance,
but to do what lies clearly at hand.
—Thomas Carlyle

I may dream of being a saint, a president, a famous artist, or a big executive, but if the floor needs sweeping, I'd better pick up a broom and set to work. We can cry all day long about the deplorable conditions, the starvation and suffering that is rampant in other countries, yet what does it avail if the man down the block is hungry and we don't hand him some bread, or if the woman around the corner is suffering and we don't comfort her?

Our own sphere of influence may seem small, but a compassionate heart can indeed perform miracles.

Depend not on another, but lean instead on thyself.
True happiness is born of self-reliance.
—*The Laws of Manu*

Ultimately, each of us is responsible and accountable for our own life. Seek the advice and counsel of others, or that found in books or in religion, if you feel this is what is needed.

Try not to err, then, by depending on what gave you solace and comfort, what assisted you on your way.

Realize that, finally, understanding yourself, solving the riddles within, can be accomplished only within the temple of your soul.

Without you there are no teachers; without you there are no lessons; without you there is no student.

There will come a time when you believe everything is finished.
That will be the beginning.
—Louis L'Amour

The birth of day is preceded by the death of night; the end of the caterpillar is the beginning of the butterfly.

It is our fear of beginning, of rebirth, that keeps us tightly wrapped in inimical circumstances. We clutch and cling to people, ideas, places, and things in order to avoid the unknown, and so we live dispirited in an intricate web of our own making.

Mainly, we try to convince ourselves that this is what we want, the status quo, the comfortable cocoon, but deep down we truly wish to be transformed into a butterfly, a beautiful free-winged butterfly!

When all seems finished, then we will either take wing and soar, or perish in despondency.

*Living, just by itself—what a dirge that is! Life is a classroom and
boredom's the usher, there all the time to spy on you; whatever
happens, you've got to look as if you were awfully busy
all the time doing something that's terribly exciting—or he'll
come along and nibble your brain.*
—Louis-Ferdinand Céline

Boredom, that insidious character, can make people do the most
harmful things, not the least of which is abuse alcohol and drugs.
Equal to the weariness we all at times feel is the imagination we
all have. When bored, we need only employ this exciting gift to
be transported to Olympus. Indeed, idle time can be the most
creative time, for it is then that we have the opportunity to seize
the ideas that otherwise get lost in the daily shuffle.

It's not so much how busy you are, but why you are busy.
The bee is praised; the mosquito is swatted.
—Marie O'Conner

Are you busy making honey or busy sucking blood? The constant stress of activity, whether at home or abroad at work, indicates a restlessness of spirit. Forever frazzled and frantic, always cleaning or mending, fixing or building, having too much work, too much playtime scheduled after work, taking care of this and that, and oh-my-you-have-no-time-to-yourself suggest an avoidance, perhaps a fear of loneliness or a fear of facing your inner demons.

If you're the busy type, always up and about, try discovering why; and thereby you may work through to your portion of serenity.

Most people think that aging is irreversible and we know that there are mechanisms even in the human machinery that allow for the reversal of aging, through correction of diet, through antioxidants, through removal of toxins from the body, through exercise, through yoga and breathing techniques, and through meditation.
—*Deepak Chopra*

Living organisms do not go backward in time. The fountain of youth is a lovely myth, but a myth all the same. A crab grows a new arm but not a younger one. Certainly, a change in attitude and a healthier diet can make one look and feel younger. One can eat all the health food money can buy, take all the available vitamins, spread renewal creams over one's entire body, read every self-help book, and meditate all the livelong day; nonetheless, the aging process will not reverse, for it is the nature of living things to grow old and decay.

We are healed of a suffering only by experiencing it in full.
—Marcel Proust

To shun sorrow, to avoid it at all cost, is not to fully understand the nature of life. Divorce, loss, disease, and other traumas occur, and they cause suffering. This is a fact. To be clearly aware of this will lessen the blow when sorrow pays us a visit, and, alas, it will eventually pay us a visit. Avoiding the reality of sorrow serves only to intensify its effect and prolong its impact. One must see sorrow as a great teacher, and not as a great destroyer.

Oftentimes sorrow experienced squarely and in full can make the heart grow fonder.

Otherwise, sorrow can make you bitterly cynical and leave you disenchanted and broken.

Love is swift, sincere, pious, joyful, generous, strong,
patient, faithful, prudent, long-suffering, courageous,
and never seeking its own; for wheresoever a person seeketh his own,
there he falleth from love.
—*Thomas à Kempis*

Love, such a sacred and hallowed word, yet we bandy it about like a tennis ball.

If I feel no love in my heart should I then so casually use the word, or is this taking love itself in vain?

To truly love, deeply and without prejudice, surely this is a wondrous thing, a holy thing, and needs to be approached very seriously. If I say, "I love you," but feel no quickening, remain mute inwardly, does this mean I am speaking idly, simply saying what I know you want to hear? Or is what I say true because I believe I love you?

One must find out what it means to love or else take the chance of mistaking infatuation and desire for love. Or is this how you find out—by taking the chance, making mistakes?

I think, as usual, the answer resides in our own breast. Our hearts will define love for us; our hearts will let us know when it is genuine, if we can only listen to the rhythm.

Life's splendor forever lies in wait about each one of us
in all its fullness, but veiled from view, deep down, invisible,
far off. It is there, though, not hostile, not reluctant, not deaf.
If you summon it by the right word,
by its right name, it will come.
—Franz Kafka

What's the right name, the right word that we may use to call forth life's splendor: God, Spirit, Soul, Atman, Zeus, Yahweh, Beauty, Nature, or something else? Well, I suppose that depends on you, depends on where you're from and what you think and feel. Life's splendor answers to many names in many languages and at any moment in any season. With this single proviso, we must at least summon it before it will answer.

There are some people that if they don't know,
you can't tell 'em.
—Louis Armstrong

Sometimes, while treading life's path, it's best to simply walk by certain people.

Sometimes, while treading life's path, it's best to simply step aside and let certain people pass by.

Sometimes, while treading life's path, it's best to turn one's back.

The situation will dictate which of these alternatives to take.

Compassion, betimes, may mean saying, "What has thou to do with me?"

DAY 217 ✦ Riches

The only wealth is life.
—Henry David Thoreau

An infinite mine of opulent stars enrich the night.
An affluence of multifoliate greens colors the earth.
A lavish sapphire paints the seas.
The richest flowery fragrances permeate the air.
Velvet-clad animals scamper about the golden landscape.
The plush songs of birds endow the streets and forests with
    song.
Trees endowed with succulent fruit grow in backyards and
    groves.

What is a big bank account compared to all this? Indeed, the
only wealth is life—and we are all of independent means.

Weaknesses

*You cannot run away from a weakness; you must sometimes fight
it out or perish. And if that be so, why not now,
and where you stand?*
—Robert Louis Stevenson

Our weaknesses have a terrible habit of appearing from within at the most inopportune times. They lurk just under the surface until the occasion arises for them to make their presence felt, and before we can say "boo" there they are to annoy, betray, and otherwise embarrass us. That we frequently succumb to them shows their strength. Indulging in, or escaping from, our weaknesses seems only to give them more sway in our lives. Yet we persist in not dealing with them until they assume a monstrous stature.

Why not stand and fight the good fight with them now when they are smaller and more manageable?

Through pride we are ever deceiving ourselves. But deep down below
the surface of the average conscience a still, small voice says
to us, "Something is out of tune."
—Carl Jung

We are the great pretenders. Out into the streets we go with our
egos out in front as buffers. We place them there to give everyone
we meet the impression that our life is just grand. But we know
different. Deep down we know it's the same old song and dance.

Our mental rhythms are discordant. The clang and clatter of
our thoughts, the dissonance of our subconscious mind indicates
that something is out of tune. We need to restring our instruments
to be in sync with that "still, small voice."

First, we must allow that we're out of tune, then we must
be willing to work at getting in tune. Only then may we play
beautiful music.

Work like you don't need the money.
Dance like no one is watching.
And love like you've never been hurt.
—Mark Twain

In other words, act freely, without self-consciousness but with self-assurance and reverence. Carry your tap shoes over your shoulder and whistle a tune on the way to the dance studio. Once there, dance like only the mirrors are watching.

That you've been hurt in love is not unusual but rather common; in fact it's a universal and timeless experience. Seeing to it that the poison of your first or last heartbreak does not maliciously infect your new relationship, this is something new.

Be aware, yet not wearied; be open, yet not naïve; be wanting, yet not needy.

Love is a renewal and thus requires that we come to it new, each time.

*In every man's heart there is a secret nerve
that answers to the vibrations of beauty.*
—Christopher Morley

Beauty tapped me on the shoulder yesterday, and I turned to see a nearly full moon lingering in a pale blue sky. I said beauty tapped me on the shoulder yesterday, and I saw lingering in a pale blue sky a nearly full moon.

Beauty's quiver pierced me and I turned to see one of her faces, and I'm grateful for the vision.

I'm thankful for seeing that soundless symphony.

After all this time, to still be astonished by such a sight, to still be invigorated by nature's unerring appeal, to feel emboldened by its ever fresh approach, this is truly the blessedness of beauty.

I found thee not, O Lord, without, because I erred in seeking thee
without that wert within.
—*Saint Augustine*

I know people who have spent a lifetime believing—praying, attending church regularly, and faithfully practicing their religion's precepts—and yet are no closer to God than is the man on the corner who hasn't set foot in a church in twenty years.

The light is in your eyes as well as in the stained-glass windows. The altar may sit in yonder meadow and the chalice may be in your cupboard, but to find out you must indeed seek within.

To avoid criticism do nothing, say nothing, be nothing.
—Elbert Hubbard

I'm afraid this statement is not entirely accurate. I know people who have tried this and they too were criticized—criticized for doing, saying, and being nothing.

Stand up and be counted. Criticism is unavoidable and can at times be beneficial. Part of our humanness is the critical capacity of our minds. This faculty is what enables us to distinguish, discover, and create. The ability to think critically, this is an important ability, one that deserves our attention.

Used properly, the proper dose given at the proper time, criticism can be of value. Of course petty and vindictive criticisms like "I don't like you" or "You're an idiot" are destructive, not to mention cruel. But true criticism, true criticism promotes growth.

Though we may at first balk even at constructive criticism, it's usually worthwhile to take a second look to see whether the criticism has any merit; and if it does, well, we should be thankful rather than offended.

Life is not so short but that there is always time for courtesy.
—Ralph Waldo Emerson

To hold open a door; to say "thank you" and "you're welcome," "hello" and "good-bye";

To inquire into the welfare of your neighbor; to ask politely instead of rudely demand;

To let a car out of a driveway; to pick up after yourself; to be forbearing and friendly;

To be civil and refined; to carry yourself with dignity and grace; to offer your hand in help;

To be kind and courteous; to be amiable and considerate; to be cordial and indulgent, magnanimous and just plain decent, surely we have "world enough and time" for this.

DAY 225 ✦ Choices

*I will not be as those who spend the day in complaining of headache,
and the night in drinking the wine that gives it.*
—Johann Wolfgang von Goethe

Life is full to the brim of complaints and ailments. But from
whence do we complain and from what do we ail? Our own
poor choices drive us to bitter complaints, while our own careless
indulgences provide us with chronic ailments.

Continue, if you must, making ill-advised decisions; continue,
if you must, indulging your every whim, but know that such
actions have consequences, and at least be willing to unflinchingly
accept the inevitable headaches.

My mind is my own church.
—*Thomas Paine*

The temple is within, along with all the sacred texts. You need only find the entranceway to your soul; you need only know how to translate the wisdom of your heart.

In the church of your own mind you may worship, confess, do penance, and preach. In addition, you may receive the divine blessing and be anointed with grace.

The mind is vast, more spacious than the grandest cathedrals. It is up to each one of us to explore this immense holy space. It is up to each one of us to find the secret scrolls within.

*If you would be a real seeker after truth, it is necessary
that at least once in your life you doubt,
as far as possible, all things.*
—René Descartes

To be sure, a healthy sense of doubt, an eagerness and ability to question our most fundamental beliefs and opinions, leads us toward self-discovery. If we never question, never doubt, we are essentially living our lives on borrowed thoughts. Living conditioned lives, we know not from whence we speak, and know not from whence we think.

Certainly, it is part of our birthright to doubt and to question. By doubting and questioning we may stumble upon truths hidden by those habits of thought, that endless repetition that makes up our consciousness. And once we discover a truth in this doubtful manner, through our uncertainty, our open-minded diligence, it becomes a part of us.

A noble man compares and estimates himself by an idea which
is higher than himself; and a mean man, by one lower
than himself. The one produces aspiration; the other ambition,
which is the way in which a vulgar man aspires.
—Joseph Conrad

No one could ever accuse Mother Teresa of being ambitious. Ambition is for businessmen and politicians. She aspired to be worthy of her calling, to minister to the sick and hungry, and she was thus ennobled.

Aspiring (from the Latin *aspiro*, "breath upon") has more to do with spirit, whereas ambition (from the Latin *ambitio*, "go around") has more to do with ego.

The aspirant is intent upon transcendence, while the ambitious are out for personal gain. The former is driven by love and the latter are driven by the desire for power. The ambitious will destroy to get what they want as the aspirant builds to get what he or she must.

Today we hear much talk about ambition and too little about aspiration; we applaud the one and ignore the other. Perhaps after understanding the difference we will aspire to great heights rather than inordinately desire status.

No one ever won a chess game by betting on each move. Sometimes you have to move backward to get a step forward.
—Amar Gopal Bose

What's the point of labeling every misstep as a failure? Why not consider mistakes as lessons and let one step backward equal two steps forward? Unfortunately, the game will continue in spite of our becoming disheartened. This is one game where quitting is of no value whatsoever.

Has your marriage been dissolved? Surely the love you shared early on means something to you now. Did you have children? Surely they are beautiful and made the whole thing worthwhile.

Disappointments are as common as pawns and the true failure lies not in setbacks, but in living your life with bitter regrets. Sometimes life requires of us that we give something up before we get something else, and there's always a something else.

The game is not over until the final move has been made.

Water is the principle, or the element, of things.
—*Thales of Miletus*

Listen to the water—the river, stream, or ocean—for it will teach you many things.

It will teach you about ebb and flow. It will teach you about staying afloat and going under.

It will teach you about persistence and the path of least resistance, and about cleansing and purification.

It will teach you about surfaces and depths. It will teach you that the earth and sky are indivisible. More than all this, it will teach you about change, about sustaining life and death.

Stop a moment, cease your work, and look around you.
—Thomas Carlyle

What do you see? A butterfly on the wing, a tree in bloom, the shadows on the wall, an endearing smile, a lonely road, a desperate measure, a lover's appeal, the angel-blue sky, your dexterous fingers, the tips of your shoes or the top of a mountain, tonight's meal or yesterday's book, the heartbreak, the despair, the joy, the revelation—come, cease your work for a moment, and tell us what you see.

It is always in season for old men to learn.
—Aeschylus

Wisdom is ageless. One needs only look at a child to see an inherent wisdom, a timeless clarity. Alas, too many of us never learn from experience; too many of us pass through the years repeating the same mistakes, never deviating from our lonely roads, and so grow old and foolish. Never having contemplated, never having reflected on a different way, we get and stay in a rut until we find ourselves old, embittered, and disgusted. We fail to see that the childlike wisdom, the vitality and freshness that once resided in us, still resides in us, no matter our age.

For old age to be bearable we need young and active minds, and a mind that is young and active has the capacity for wonder. Not, "I wonder if my arthritis will act up today," but rather, "I wonder what new wonders this day will have in store?"

I hold it true, whate'er befall;
I feel it, when I sorrow most;
'Tis better to have loved and lost
Than never to have loved at all.
—*Alfred, Lord Tennyson*

Trying to love without risk, without the possibility of suffering, is like trying to kiss without touching lips. In order to get the full flavor of love, we must be willing to give ourselves entirely. Once stung by Cupid's arrow, we are as vulnerable as kittens, and this is as it should be. Why cheat yourself? Why live in half measures, and thereby remain unavailable to some of life's most telling lessons?

Will you get hurt? Possibly. But you will also have truly loved and lived.

We shall always and ever embrace the entire movement of love, including the suffering, as love requires this of us—as does suffering.

Love seeketh not itself to please,
Nor for itself hath any care,
But for another gives its ease,
And builds a Heaven in Hell's despair.
—William Blake

You see now, lying alone on the blistering sand,
Feeling the feverish abscess of despair,
That when you think yourself to please, love,
Displeased, vanishes into thin air.

Love, which seeketh and asketh nothing but to be;
Love, which comes and goes unbidden,
That finest and most privileged mystery.

DAY 235 ◆ Life Stories

The universe is made of stories, not atoms.
—*Muriel Rukeyser*

The stories of love and triumph, tragedy and despair, supply the chapters for the book of our lives. Each of us has a story worthy of Homer; each of us has lived, at the very least, an inner life replete with all the adventures of epic stories. Loyalty, betrayal, fear, courage, love, and suffering—who among us hasn't experienced these things?

All of us know the sorrows of Penelope, the torments of Lancelot, and the buffoonery and incredulity of Sancho Panza. This is why we still understand and appreciate the *Odyssey;* the adventures of King Arthur; or, more to the point, the poignant searching of Don Quixote.

To be sure, our lives are a story, a memorable story filled with incredible adventure. Because no one chooses to write about it doesn't make it any less a momentous journey.

The true test of civilization is, not the census,
nor the size of cities, nor the crops
but the kind of man that the country turns out.
—Ralph Waldo Emerson

Ancient Athens (Socrates, Pythagoras, Plato, Sappho, Aristotle), Renaissance Italy (da Vinci, Michelangelo, Brunelleschi, Raphael), Enlightenment France (Voltaire, Rousseau, Diderot), and Constitutional America (Jefferson, Franklin, Paine) are just a few of the examples of times and civilizations that turned out a special crop of people. Of course, a contrary list could be made of times and civilizations that turned out a poisoned crop of people. So the question of what type of people our civilization is turning out remains to be seen. Wise, creative, and iconoclastic people, or dogmatic, dull, and superficial people? When answering, keep in mind the phrase "We the people," because we—you and I—are the people.

I repeat to myself, slowly and soothingly,
a list of quotations beautiful from minds profound—
if I can remember any of the damn things.
—Dorothy Parker

Such a wit, that Dorothy Parker! Another gentle reminder that repeating beautiful and profound quotations, without understanding their inherent meaning, is as useful as repeatedly quoting a recipe. She understood that memorizing the deep and profound was fruitless, because it was easily forgotten. Better by far to think problems out for ourselves and own thereby the answers than to needlessly struggle with memorizing the profound in what amounts to vain attempts to appear clever.

Don't close your eyes; plagiarize.
—Anonymous

Steal everything into your eyes. Take all the available light and allow your mind to translate it into form. Absorb into yourself the sad and beautiful, the delightful and ugly—the tears in the rain and the perspiration of sunbeams. Plunder with your eyes the world's treasures. Rob the sunlight as well as the moonlight. Leave nothing unobserved: neither the ant scurrying in the grass, nor the clouds relaxing over the mountain; neither the dreams whispering in your sleep, nor your neighbor's quiet loneliness.

*Neither a lofty degree of intelligence nor imagination nor
both together go to the making of genius.
Love, love, love, that is the soul of genius.*
—*Wolfgang Amadeus Mozart*

Only a lover could have composed such intelligent, imaginative,
and rarified music. Only the energy love provides would suffice
to sustain such a prodigious creative output. Without love embracing the artist in a swoon of creativity, he is but a "gong and
clanging symbol." Like a lover courting his beloved, the intoxi-
cated artist throws himself passionately into his work, and the
result is a symphony. Intelligence and imagination come to nothing when love is not there to bestow delicacy and sensitivity.

Expect poison from the standing water.
—*William Blake*

That which doesn't flow, course like a stream down the mountainside, around and over rocks, ever pushing and pulsing, ever moving and adapting, ever taking its rough or gentle way through summer and winter, ever refreshing, and sustaining in its quest to mix with the ocean is as stagnant water, gathering to itself noxious bacteria born of inaction, and is an anathema to the living, the pulsating, the flowing.

Anger blows out the lamp of the mind.
—Robert G. Ingersoll

Let it go . . . just let it go. I'll say it again, let it go.

Whatever bitterness, whatever enmity you harbor, I say to you, let it go, release it into the wind.

Whatever hatred, whatever obsession haunts your daily life, I ask you, please, let it go, release it into the river.

Whatever malevolence, whatever rancor obscures your vision and blackens the world, I urge you to let it go, let it go now, so that you may see clearly again.

Leave it, as it was never yours to keep to begin with.

*Never doubt that a small group of thoughtful citizens can change
the world. Indeed, it is the only thing that ever has.*
—*Margaret Mead*

Both great and terrible events start with a few, sometimes only
one. Jesus and his Disciples, Hitler and his followers, Buddha and
his disciples, Pol Pot and his followers, Muhammad and his faithful, Moses and his tribes, all significantly altered not only the
outward face of the world, but also the inner space of the world.
A new idea can spread through human consciousness like a wildfire. Some of these ideas are beneficent, while others are
iniquitous.

To each of us is given the responsibility of governing our own
minds, of sorting out for ourselves those ideas that enhance the
world and those that degrade it.

Don't just accept, but question, using your own conscience
as arbiter.

Man needs difficulties.
They are necessary for health.
—Carl Jung

Show me a person without difficulties, and I'll show you a zombie. Life is replete with challenges and we are equipped to meet those challenges.

What would happen to our imagination without obstacles? Would there even be any bridges if someone, somewhere, at some time, didn't have difficulty crossing a river?

Difficulties are par for the course, and generally each of us is not given more than we can bear.

It's not the difficulties themselves, however, or that there are difficulties, but how we handle them that speaks to our mental health. Do we become enraged and throw a fit when we meet with difficulties, or do we set to work with our minds to solve the problems?

Unfortunately, how we handle ourselves during life's travails depends largely upon our upbringing, when it should depend on our understanding, on the light that we are able to summon to illuminate life's inevitable difficulties, on our willingness to look and see and learn.

Eternity is not something that begins after you are dead.
It is going on all the time.
We are in it now.
—Charlotte Gilman

Eternity—that sense of timelessness, the feeling of being completely present. Most of us experience it only on certain uninvited occasions, such as beholding the sunset, observing the moonlight on the ocean, listening to the rainfall, or eyeing that special someone walking down the street. What name do we give these eternal moments? Beauty. Beauty is the name of eternity and the eternal. And where hides this elusive beauty? It's on the couch next to you. It's hanging on the wall behind you. It's under the rock in your front yard. Look, it's going on all the time.

The falling drops at last will wear the stone.
—Lucretius

With patience we may yet conquer our most difficult problems.

With patience we may yet endure the weightiest of difficulties.

With patience we may yet be forbearing to those that understand not what they do.

With patience we may yet learn to love properly.

With patience we may yet learn to live with some portion of serenity.

With patience we may yet learn to act at last with a spirit hitherto unknown to us.

A man who suffers before it is necessary
suffers more than what is necessary.
—*Seneca*

By anticipating suffering we double its dose. Furthermore, it often happens that anticipated suffering creates more pain than the actual event we fear.

Things often aren't as bad as we can think them, and much needless torment is caused by our projections.

No use in forecasting suffering. We should enjoy the fair weather while it lasts. When it rains, it rains, and sometimes you can't avoid getting wet. Only a fool carries his umbrella with him all year long. Besides, lingering behind every storm cloud is the sun, and the sun will always out.

DAY 247 ✦ Contentment

*He who is not contented with what he has, would not be
contented with what he would like to have.*
—Socrates

So your house is too small, your car is too slow, and your dish-
washer is too old.

You'd like to upgrade to the latest and greatest, and then you
will be satisfied.

As soon as you get that promotion, life will be grand.

When you fall in love and get married, everything will be for
the best.

A child, that's what's missing; children will make your life
complete.

If you save enough then you can retire early, and really begin
to enjoy your life.

See a pattern?

Life Is Full of Surprises

Surprise is the greatest gift which life can grant us.
—*Boris Pasternak*

Surprise, you're in love.
Surprise, the sun broke through the clouds.
Surprise, it's your birthday.
Surprise, there is snow on the mountain peaks.
Surprise, will you marry me?
Surprise, it's a full moon.
Surprise, you are pregnant.
Surprise, you just saw a shooting star.
Surprise, your son or daughter just graduated from college.
Surprise, life is renewed daily.
Surprise, you've just learned something new.
Surprise, surprise, surprise!

There's nothing remarkable about it. All one has to do is hit the right keys at the right time and the instrument plays itself.
—*Johann Sebastian Bach*

Our body, the instrument, also plays itself, has its own harmonies and rhythms. When in tune, it plays melodiously, a symphony of sensuous perfection that carries throughout the world a song for the ages, a piece for posterity—a man or a woman.

This self-tuning, self-conducting instrument plays from the music sheet of existence the notes of life, and we need only see to it that this remarkable instrument is well taken care of, properly polished and tuned, handled gently and with respect, so that it may sound exquisite in any concert hall.

DAY 250 ✦ Living

How we spend our days is, of course,
how we spend our lives.
—Annie Dillard

You rouse yourself in the morning, have a little breakfast, and then make your way to work.

You spend a few hours at your job, then go to lunch.

After lunch, you spend a few more hours at work, and then you drive home.

At home, you eat dinner, then relax in front of the television until it's time for bed.

After a bit of sleep you get up and do it all over again.

One can only hope that you work at something you love.

All changes, even the most longed for, have their melancholy;
for what we leave behind us is a part of ourselves;
we must die to one life before we can enter another.
—Anatole France

Inevitably we will experience some despondency, if not agony, when we end a relationship. Despite how troubling the relationship has become and how appropriate the decision to say enough and no more, we invariably feel the sting of finality.

We fear to lose what we've become because of this relationship, and are anxious about who we will become without this relationship.

After all, we gave considerably of ourselves, and also changed considerably engaged in this affair. But these pangs we feel are as birth pangs toward our new life, and so have their purpose and import, and have their own beauty, and hold their own unexpected promise.

*Adversity has ever been considered the state in which a man
most easily becomes acquainted with himself.*
—Samuel Johnson

Adversity, the great teacher, expounds on sorrow.

Adversity, the great teacher, lectures on fear, anxiety, and distress.

Adversity, the great teacher, tutors on love.

Adversity, the great teacher, gives lessons on compassion, fortitude, and equanimity.

Adversity, the great teacher, daily tests our resolve.

Adversity, the great teacher, drags us kicking and screaming to the mirror.

Adversity, the great teacher, heightens our senses and sharpens our minds, and it falls to us, its students, to get acquainted with its rigorous curriculum.

At the touch of love everyone becomes a poet.
—Plato

Love never ends, though it may temporarily disregard us. Like a fragrant flower that is redolent to all that pass it by, anyone with an open heart is susceptible to love. We're never too old for "that nonsense."

Love is forever in bloom and we the bees delight in its nectar. At times our noses may be stuffy and our wings clipped, but the former will clear and the latter will grow back and soon we will be back buzzing in the bedazzled garden.

Have faith in love and it will have faith in you. Passion lives in the wind and we are its favored creatures. Mark well your heartbeats, for they are timed for love. A caress from the poignant eyes of a hitherto stranger may be all it takes to send you aloft in a fit of lyrical ecstasy. Spread out, make room for the muse of beauty; she may just want to sit next to you!

Each friend represents a world in us, a world possibly not born
until they arrive, and it is only by this meeting
that a new world is born.
—Anaïs Nin

When we happen upon a person who will be a friend, we recognize that person immediately, not only because of the instant and easy rapport, but also because of something unnameable, something intangible, like the birth of a star that says this is a kindred spirit, a brother in the wilderness, a lamp in the house of Usher.

With a friend all things are possible. We can argue, laugh, cry, and even act the fool with no one quite so often and so well as we can with a friend. Our friends are our selves in a different guise, integral pieces of the maddening puzzle.

A day without friends is no day at all, but a lonely, anguished night.

Hold fast to your friends, for without friendship the world would perish.

Whoever gossips to you will gossip about you.
—Spanish proverb

Idle gossip is not idle, but insidious. People with soap opera mouths spend their time spreading intrigue and suspicion, and no one is safe from their meddling prattle. To be sure, if a busybody tells you all about Sue, he will tell Sue all about you. What's more, those most shocked by such a betrayal are usually the gossips themselves. A strange bunch indeed. Bored and dissatisfied, they thrive on the troubles of others.

Keep in mind next time someone wants to tell you a rumor that one good gossip does not deserve another.

Respect another's privacy and that person will respect yours.

Who's the Fairest of Them All?

His face was filled with broken commandments.
—John Masefield

We need only look into the mirror to see there reflected the saga of our life.

Too many days in the sun? Ah, those wrinkles tell the tale.

A 1,001 restless nights? The baggy eyes say as much.

Cynical to the core, finally? That sardonic smile professes it.

Given over to anger and resentment? A tensely furrowed brow doesn't lie.

Lonely and afraid? It's all there in those vague, troubled eyes.

The face is the repository of our life story. Despite our different moods and various disguises, we at long last can't help but wear the countenance we have lived.

No one worth possessing can be quite possessed.
—Sara Teasdale

Love delights in liberty and thus abhors possession. Possession—or attempts to possess—smothers love.

Love needs space in which to breathe and thrive. The irony is that those we would most like to possess are the ones most likely to resist possession. Though they don't resist love, the self-sustained resist being shackled. The abode of love is freedom and generosity of spirit and those who understand this have wings—and by their very nature such winged ones cannot be possessed.

To those for whom love is but a pillow to lay their weary heads, these find only disenchantment.

To those for whom love is but filler for an inner void, these find within an unappeasable jealousy.

To those for whom love is but an opiate, and so go from one fix to another, these find in the end only loneliness and bitterness.

Love delights in liberty.

DAY 258 ✦ Fantasy

An object in possession seldom retains the same
charm that it had in pursuit.
—*Pliny the Younger*

For many of us it's the thrill and excitement of the hunt, the racing over hill and dale in pursuit of an elusive quarry, that holds all the allure. Once captured, our prey quickly loses its mystery and fascination, they being replaced by an awful familiarity.

And then we feel betrayed. And we were betrayed, betrayed by our own imagination, an imagination gone awry, an imagination that sought itself to please and couldn't see the forest for the trees.

We get so caught up in fantasy and projection that when we do finally possess we find ourselves holding only disappointment, an "it's not what I expected it to be," not realizing that, if given a proper chance, reality is much more interesting.

DAY 259 ◆ The First Step

Where shall we begin? There is no beginning. Start where you arrive.
Stop before what entices you. And work! You will enter
little by little into the entirety. Method will be born
in proportion to your interest.
—Auguste Rodin

Anywhere we start is the beginning. Thinking too much about the middle and the end can be so daunting it can leave us paralyzed. Sometimes it's wise just to begin and let the task itself guide us to its fruition.

Once we've begun, diligence and patience allows us to keep pace with our work, despite distractions and delays, despite doubt and insecurity, until soon the work itself takes on its own life, creates its own form, and we become its sustaining passion.

Life beats down and crushes the soul and art
reminds you that you have one.
—*Stella Adler*

The beauty and unity of the soul, all its divinity and mystery, should be what's revealed or intimated in a great work of art. This is the test of its truth. Though tastes change and generations pass, a work of art remains what it was when it was created—it remains an articulation of the universal soul.

Thankfully, the fecund earth continues to give birth to artists. These spiritual visionaries, these missionaries of creative passion, continue to reveal what life's brutal aspect at times conceals; namely, that essence we call the soul of life.

And we should be thankful that, even if we don't create, at least we can still appreciate.

To oppose something is to maintain it.
—Ursula K. Le Guin

The effort to oppose gives strength and durability to that which we would abolish. By utilizing our mental energies to combat those thoughts or feelings that afflict us, we unwittingly are giving them more presence and power. Our resistance makes them redouble their efforts. One thought provokes another and so the inward battle is joined. Whereas, if we don't antagonize those oppressive thoughts and feelings, if we can watch them without engagement, and not stir them with the arms of opposition, then they usually will withdrawal of themselves.

Without a viable opponent a duelist soon retreats from the field.

It is easier to be wise for others than for ourselves.
—La Rochefoucauld

Why is it that we seem to be able to provide the most sage advice to others and not to ourselves? We tell our friends exactly how and what they should do in a given situation, and our counsel seems so wise and true, we are flabbergasted when they don't follow our ageless guidance.

Yet when we find ourselves in a pickle, we look for all the world models of confusion and indecisiveness, and presently take our spot in the advice line. Does the reason lie with our relative detachment from the one circumstance and our complete immersion in the other? After all, don't most situations seem simple when they're no hardship to us?

Perhaps we could give ourselves the same free advice we so casually give to others if we could but step back a moment and view our own predicaments with more detachment.

If the bird does like its cage, and does like its sugar, and will not
leave it, why keep the door so very carefully shut?
—Olive Schreiner

Beautiful cages and the alluring enticements we know are fleeting, and as we don't quite trust enough in love itself, we put what we love behind an emotional lock and key, so, we believe, this will secure them to us.

Unlock the door and throw away the key. Allow your birds all the freedom they can have and if they should decide to test the expanse of their wings, then think only about how much longing they must have had for the blue sky. Think also about how cruel it is to keep what doesn't want to be kept, and how insensitive it is to clip the wings of those that would soar.

The Holy One . . . requires the heart.
—Talmud

Yes, the heart, because thought won't get us there. Indeed, thought hinders and baffles where the Holy One is concerned. Our approach to the Holy One requires a mind free from the burden of thinking. It's in the silence between thoughts that we meet what is holy.

We may read the Bible a thousand times and the Talmud a thousand more and yet not feel the presence of the Holy One.

A strange set of affairs, this seeking. After years spent straining and studying, we can, curiously enough, be further from the truth than the man who walks out his door at dawn, and looks over his shoulder at the lone oriole singing on the bough of a walnut tree, and is filled by this vision with an indescribable ecstasy.

Give a man a fish and you feed him for a day.
Teach a man to fish and you feed him for a lifetime.
—Chinese proverb

It's no use living on borrowed knowledge. We must understand matters, both practical and spiritual, for ourselves. We may think we know something and come to find we had only a superficial knowledge of it based on a reading or a discussion. We didn't truly understand; we didn't experience it "with our bones."

Real learning is more about the insight of understanding than it is about knowledge. Though of course knowledge plays an important part in both learning and in life—after all, we couldn't drive a car or read a book without knowledge—it is not the vital part. The most useful truths come to us by way of flashes of insight, an inscrutable kind of learning that penetrates deep into the heart and is unrelated to memorization. To understand things in this manner is to experience living truth.

*To find out your real opinion of someone, judge the impression
you have when you first see a letter from him.*
—*Arthur Schopenhauer*

At first glance this may seem like a facile suggestion. But on further reflection we can see its psychological depth. With the proliferation of E-mail and the omnipresence of phones, we can easily test its truth. Our first impressions, those pre-thought feelings we have when we first answer the phone or open the mail, tend to be our most genuine. Is it with chagrin or excitement that we register his or her voice on the line? Do we see that person's name in our in-box and respond with an "oh, no" or an "oh, yes"? Before thought arrives with its excuses and rationalizations, our initial impressions, however fleeting, spell out for us in no uncertain terms our true feelings.

It is in our idleness, in our dreams, that the submerged
truth sometimes comes to the top.
—*Virginia Woolf*

Our conscious mind may reason, but our subconscious mind dis-covers. Insight imbibes from the deepest wells, but if you are forever mending the cup you will never be refreshed. To catch the subtle signals that emerge from the reservoir of the mind requires attentiveness not usually found in the common, busy day-light hours. In the repose of idleness and dreams come the intima-tions of truth.

We need only remain awake enough to sense them.

We need only allow ourselves the leisure to be awake.

DAY 268 ◆ Duality

Out beyond ideas of right-doing and wrong-doing
there is a field. I'll meet you there.
—Jalāl ad-Din ar-Rūmī

Field of vision . . . entering a new field . . . a field of dreams. . . . force field . . . love field . . . field notes. . . . field the stars along with the ball . . .

Perhaps each of us will one day—before our last day—find our way into this mystic field. Once we put this world of duality to rest, we may see in an entirely new way, and so begin to live with quite a different vision, in a different field of consciousness. Until such time, we must content ourselves with coming to grips with our world of right and wrong, of good and bad. Starting from here, we may yet get there.

Religion is a candle inside a multicolored lantern. Everyone looks through a particular color, but the candle is always there.
—Muhammad Neguib

Despite beliefs, theories, dogmas, and rhetoric, the flame of truth perpetually burns. Each religion claims the sanctity of spiritual truth and each in its way partakes of this truth. However, those in the religious community that insist that their particular belief is the one and only path to godliness, those are the most distant from the religious spirit. The religious spirit is an inclusive, embracing spirit, and not a divisive, exclusionary spirit. Like the candle flame, which shares its luminance equally to all those who would avail themselves of it, so glows the truly religious spirit.

God enters by a private door into every individual.
—Ralph Waldo Emerson

No two doors to the ground of being are the same. To each of us comes the responsibility of finding his or her own key. The divine spirit may appear to us at any time and under any circumstance. We need only to extend an invitation and then leave the door ajar. Otherwise, we sense only from time to time a vague knocking which we quickly learn to ignore. Hopefully, when you hear that tap, tap, tapping on your private door, you'll have the courage and the key to open it.

DAY 271 ✦ Kindness

Three things in human life are important.
The first is to be kind. The second is to be kind.
And the third is to be kind.
—Henry James

The kindness and the heartfelt solicitude of those we know and love, and of those we don't yet know and may yet love, create within us a peaceful sanctuary of goodwill. Before long this little bower within begins to bloom with color and fragrance and spreads out like a million flower petals caught in a breeze in an ever-widening, ever-generous circle of fellowship.

Kindness is contagious.

One act of kindness inspires another, kind to kind.

Remember this the next time an opportunity to be kind presents itself.

When it gets dark enough you can see the stars.
—*Lee Salk*

At times we need to experience the darkest depths of despair before we can see clearly. Most substance abusers will tell you that they finally realized they needed help only after reaching the very dregs of addictive degradation. Only at this blackest point of despair and futility did they hear that whispering from the depths, that call to awareness—a call back toward life and the vast mystery and beauty of the stars and everything under them. Sometimes we need to go all the way down before we can get back up. And it often happens that those who arise from the lowest points end standing tallest.

DAY 273 ✦ The Dance of Life

*In the end we shall have had enough of cynicism and skepticism and
humbug and we shall want to live more musically.*
—Vincent van Gogh

Why wait till the end? Shall we dance? Shall we sing? Yes, of
course, dancing and singing time is now. This shouldn't be post-
poned. The music won't allow it. Your feet begin to tap, and your
lips start to quiver: When the rhythm infects you, you must dance;
and when the melody catches you, you must sing. This is the law
of living musically.

Plenty of odd days will there be when your feet won't budge
and your lips won't open, and any amount of music shall leave
you flat.

So be sure to sing and dance—though it is only in your soul—
on the even days.

DAY 274 ✦ Desire

You want freedom from the bitter fruits of desire, not from desire itself, and this is a very important thing to understand.
—Krishnamurti

What we want is blameless desire; desire devoid of consequences. However, the very nature of desire itself—with its longings, disappointments, and fulfillments—has its own ineluctable movement.

To covet, to want, to prize, remands us to a merry-go-round of pain and pleasure. Sometimes we get what we want and are happy. Sometimes we don't get what we want and are sad. Sometimes we get what we want and are miserable. Sometimes we don't get what we want and are better off. So understanding the process of desire, rather than wishing only to have this pleasurable desire and not that painful desire, is the issue.

Our particular desires may vary, but the nature of desire remains the same for everyone.

Money often costs too much.
—*Ralph Waldo Emerson*

Single-mindedly pursuing the false god of money is too expensive to the spirit. This is not to say that we should all embrace poverty and head for a cave in the mountains, but only to say that we should consider moderation in money matters.

The quest for dollars tends to be all-consuming and leaves little time for anything else: Chasing after coins our minds become preoccupied without becoming enriched; chasing after coins our purses may swell, but our humanity shrinks; chasing after coins broadens our desires while constricting our hearts; chasing after coins, we acquire many acquaintances, but have no true friends, and at the end of the day, the even-handed grave awaits alike for the prince and the pauper.

Such a profit and loss statement should be self-evident.

As long as I live, so long do I learn.
—Ramakrishna

Living and learning should be synonymous. Without continued learning, living becomes a stale and weary affair. We should consider learning as an ongoing odyssey, a journey without an end. Learning new things keeps our minds fresh and alert, young and vigorous, making each day an adventure. Through learning, we actively participate rather than mechanically operate in life. Truly, learning is as essential to our well-being as food and water and is an indivisible part of living.

The fewer words the better the prayer.
—Martin Luther

A verbose dissertation on your wants, a nagging and begging will not do. Praying this way displays an uncouth selfishness, a complete immersion in your own ego. Passion, passion and simplicity, that's what's wanted in prayer. To say, "I love you, God, and I humbly ask you to walk with me through the days," may suffice. Much more could be considered an indulgence.

Allow yourself the freedom of heartfelt prayer and take the time to discover a prayer befitting your life.

If nothing else, a succinct and epigrammatic prayer will serve to focus your mind.

DAY 278 ✦ Virtue

Civilization has been thrust upon me . . . and it has not added one
whit to my love for truth, honesty, and generosity.
—*Luther Standing Bear*

Truth, honesty, and generosity do not require "civilization." Indeed, it does seem that modern civilization cheapens these virtues. One sees a paucity of these attributes in the more "civilized" societies; whereas, in the so-called primitive societies, they are prevalent. It is the intimate and harmonious nature of the tribe that allows for the cultivation of such virtues, while the displacement and fear engendered by living in modern cities promotes their deterioration. A love for truth, honesty, and generosity starts with the family, spreads to the tribe, and is easily lost in the city.

DAY 279 ✦ Divine Words

Every creature is a word of God.
—*Meister Eckehart*

God's diverse dictionary is the universe. Each plant, planet, chemical, mineral, insect, animal, mountain, star, and flower is a singular expression of the divine word. It is through his myriad creatures that God creates his language and writes the story of the world. As the expressive artists of the divine will, with us resides the responsibility of not only translating this ever-expanding book, but also of respecting every one of its words as a unique and sacred expression.

The devil can cite the Scripture for his purpose.
—William Shakespeare

An ambitious and dishonest person can twist the most profound expressions for his or her selfish ends. A slight change of context and most ideas can be used to propound a fallacious or divisive point. This is why it is important that when we listen to others, especially those in positions of authority, we consider not only what is being said, but also who is saying it, and for what purpose.

Life is filled with charlatans and hucksters that can mangle and deform the words and ideas of others for personal gain, and some monks may only be new age con men in suits, trickster coyotes in disguise.

Self-Purification

Purity and impurity depend on oneself.
No one can purify another.
—Buddha

This thought expresses not only the essential "aloneness" of our lives, but also the weighty responsibility we all share as human beings. To set aside reliance on another, and stand completely alone, is a very difficult thing for us to do.

We tend to use others to fill the lonely places in our hearts. We oftentimes rely heavily on family, lovers, and friends to fix what inwardly ails us. But escaping into the seeming sanctuary of another causes insecurity and conflict in that relationship.

To enter a relationship pure and whole, instead of impure and needy, is the only way to experience the true sanctity of relationship.

Our work continues to be self-purification.

*The beauty of the world and the orderly arrangement
of everything celestial makes us confess that there is
an excellent and eternal nature, which ought to be worshipped
and admired by all mankind.*
—*Cicero*

When people and their thoughts are involved, it is there that we find disorder and violence. The endless battles between nations, and the eternal bickering between religions, are the large-scale versions of the battles and bickering that we daily engage in.

The celestial sphere of which our planet is a part speaks of harmony and order. Indeed, the very diversity and coherence of life on our little planet signifies a masterful accordance. Such indelible natural intricacies dismiss the notion of chaos. Therefore, we should be grateful, grateful that the universe expresses such a beautiful order, and also for the privilege of being here to sense it.

The music in my heart I bore
long after it was heard no more.
—William Wordsworth

As a favorite song lives on in the mind, so does an insight once achieved play on in our consciousness. No longer an intellectual property to be recalled or simply forgotten, but now the very stuff of our blood, a symphony written on our spirit. How profoundly important, then, to develop our own understanding, our own lyric of life so that the band will play on in our hearts long after they packed it in for the evening.

How exciting and life-affirming to be your own traveling minstrel show!

Nothing is more painful than to be plunged back into the world of the past, when that past is irrevocably gone by, and a new thing far away is struggling to come to life in one.
—D. H. Lawrence

A song, a movie, a certain perfume, a face in the crowd, all potential catalysts to send us reeling into the picture show of the past. Strolling along a familiar street in autumn, the chirp of a sparrow gets you reminiscing about a bygone time when you were in love and carefree. Why did things have to go so wrong? And here you're plunged into the bitterness of regret. Here you're confronted with the irrevocable past. Meanwhile, you're still walking down the street, as the song of the sparrow grows fainter and fainter; and another chance for birthing what wants to be born inside becomes stillborn, sacrificed to the past.

Everyone takes the limits of his own vision
for the limits of the world.
—Arthur Schopenhauer

An astronomer enters the observatory and points the latest, most powerful telescope into the sky, and the universe expands. A particle physicist walks into the laboratory and turns on the latest, most powerful microscope and peers into the infinitesimal, and the universe expands. Limitless, this universe of big and small, near and far. We don't need the astronomer or the physicist, the observatory or the laboratory, to tell us this is so. Our own minds can attest to it for us. Beyond the limitations of our experience lies the spectacle of the infinite.

I think it pisses God off if you walk by the color purple
in a field somewhere and don't notice it.
—*Alice Walker*

Whether or not you care, lilacs will continue to bloom, and so will violets and orchids. Your apathy will not prevent the plum, pomegranate, or grape from ripening. Beauty will come, despite your indifference.

Life has many and mysterious ways of reminding us of itself and its beauty. Sometimes it does it with a slap, and sometimes with a kiss.

Nevertheless, it does appear that to those of us who are lethargic and unresponsive, who refuse to appreciate natural splendor wherever it may appear, life can be merciless.

You shouldn't say it is not good. You should say, you do not
like it; and then, you know, you're perfectly safe.
—James Whistler

Express your own and not another's view, no matter what authority that person claims. Is the painting a marvel of modernism?
What do you think? Maybe to you it's a marvel of confusion. If
so, say it!

Everyone considers that movie a classic piece of auteur film-
making. Well, you're not everyone. What do you think? Maybe
to you it was a classic study in boredom. If so, say it!

The book reviewer wrote a marvelous review of so-and-so's
new book. Yes . . . and? Have you yourself read it? What did
you think?

Self-observation brings man to the realization of the necessity of self-change. And in observing himself a man notices that self-observation itself brings about certain changes in his inner processes. He begins to understand that self-observation is an instrument of self-change, a means of awakening.
—Gurdjieff

Let us set sail into the uncharted waters of our mind, through the uneasy calm of our hopes and the storm of our fears, through the troubling winds of our uncertainties and desires, and onward into the murky depths of our memories. Surely this is as worthy and bold an adventure as any conceivable.

This journey is not for the timid or faint of heart, but for those seekers and creators still willing to discover. And what is there to discover? Only the vision and promise of a new world, a vast and rich inner space patiently awaiting liberation.

Home Is Where the Heart Is

*The strength of a nation derives
from the integrity of the home.*
—Confucius

A certain number of rats will live together peaceably in a box, but when you add that last one, the one that makes one too many, their once peaceful community becomes a den of destruction as the rats viciously attack each other.

In the same way, if one too many homes in a nation are in disarray, then national unrest is sure to follow.

It may sound like a cliché, but it is nonetheless true that peace and love and all that is required of a good citizenry starts in the home. Without nurturing home environments a nation is doomed, doomed to self-destruct.

So before we get ourselves involved in any number of political or social causes, let us first make sure our own homes are in order. Otherwise we are busy repainting the house while the foundation is being undermined.

The poet judges not as a judge judges but as the
sun falling around a helpless thing.
—Walt Whitman

A poet judges not by pronouncements of right but by shedding light.

A poet illuminates rather than fulminates.

A poet engages in annunciation and not denunciation.

A poet beams not screams.

A poet enlightens not frightens.

A poet doesn't gild the lawn but makes the grass golden.

*Everything has been said before, but since nobody listens we
have to keep going back and beginning all over again.*
— *André Gide*

Repetition has its place. A painter may repeat brushstrokes and
colors to great effect. In the same way, we must keep going over
the same topics, only each time we approach them, we try to do
so from a different angle, and thereby gain a different perspective.

Some of us respond more to a visceral approach, while others
to an intellectual, and still others to a combination of both. All
the same, spiritually speaking, there's nothing new under the sun,
only different ways to approach the eternal mysteries.

The lesson isn't lost on us that the Greeks reduced the entire
range of theater to just two symbols: the mask of tragedy and
the mask of comedy. Repetition has its place.

A prudent question is one-half of wisdom.
—Francis Bacon

What is love? What is truth? What is beauty? What is desire? What is fear? What is sorrow? Why am I often disenchanted? Why am I often anxious? How does one find happiness? Have you ever asked yourself these questions? Most of us have not. Yet these are the fundamental questions, the questions that lead us down the path of wisdom. Simply by asking them we take the first steps toward enlightenment. Knowing what to ask, both yourself and others, then allowing the questions to gestate within you until you become the answers is all of wisdom. This may take years or no time at all.

*I swear—by my life and my love for it—that I will never
live for the sake of another man,
nor ask another man to live for mine.*
—Ayn Rand

Independence. We all know the word. It's one of our favorites. We insist on it in our relationships. Yet we are entirely dependent on these relationships. We wear proudly our independence from relationship to relationship without pause. Yet we can't spend so much as three months on the trot by ourselves. Many of us have no idea what it means to be alone. Since we were teenagers we've been involved with one person or another and it is here that we look for and demand our independence.

So, what then is all this talk about independence? Financially independent we may well be, but emotionally independent—that is something else altogether and virtually unknown to us. Without the essential element of emotional independence, relationships quickly become unhealthy, and to live from shackle to shackle is no way to live at all.

There is no pleasure to me without communication:
there is not so much as a sprightly thought comes into my mind
that it does not grieve me to have produced alone,
and that I have no one to tell it to.
—Montaigne

When we think creatively and unearth certain truths, or when we simply feel wonderful, our state of being is such that we can't help but share our enthusiasm. Bubbling with excitement, we can't wait to tell a friend or neighbor some good news.

In the same spirit a musician will play his music, a painter will display his painting, a dancer will perform onstage, and a writer will share his words with readers—our good moods must be shared lest they go to waste.

This apportioning of our talent and joy to others through communication is vital to our well-being. It not only establishes for us a vital connection with our fellow man, but also helps to develop a mutual regard between people.

Age cannot wither her,
nor custom stale her infinite variety.
—William Shakespeare

But people and their thoughtlessness, their greed and excess can poison her soil, ravage and burn her trees, besmirch her sky, pollute her rivers and oceans, abuse and mistreat her animals, and act in an altogether inconceivably selfish and spoiled way.

Who among us wants to live in a world without the majestic tiger? Who among us wants to live in a world without the stately elephant or the regal gorilla? Shall we even discuss the fate of white rhinos, bald eagles, and wolves? What about the entire intricate ecosystem that is a rain forest? For shame, say the buffalo. For shame, say the ancient redwoods. For shame, say the wild horses. For shame, say the blue whales.

*Do you know how to digest your food? Do you know how to fill
your lungs with air? Do you know how to establish, regulate
and direct the metabolism of your body—the assimilation of
foodstuff so that it builds muscles, bones and flesh? No, you
don't know how consciously, but there is a wisdom
within you that does know.*
—Donald Curtis

Humbling, is it not, to know that our most essential functions are
not in our control? We fancy ourselves the masters of our domain,
and yet we are nothing without our bodily wisdom. When awake,
all our senses are at work despite ourselves. We can't help but
see, hear, touch, smell, and taste unless we are in a deprivation
chamber. And all the while our brains are interpreting this sensory
input, once again mostly without our assistance. Our involvement
seems to appear only with thought, and even that we can't seem
to control. If you're truly "the boss," then surely can't you stop
thinking for a moment if you wish? No, you can't. Is this because
you are your thoughts and there is no controlling thinker?

Trust in your bodily wisdom.

A crust eaten in peace is better
than a banquet partaken in anxiety.
—*Aesop*

Eating, besides being a necessity, is one of life's great delights. A well-prepared dinner that is cooked, flavored, and spiced to perfection will taste no better than gruel to the anxious mind. Whereas a mind as fully integrated as a gourmet meal can savor a meager repast of bread and water and still be thankful for the bountiful gifts of this earth.

Nothing is built on stone, all is built on sand,
but we must build as if the sand were stone.
— *Jorge Luis Borges*

That life is ephemeral, and nothing but the spirit ultimately endures, does not mean that we should become defeatist and cynical. On the contrary, we should rejoice in life's protean, evanescent nature, and build and create with a passion that trusts in the permanence of the soul and in the everlasting face of beauty. Our precious time here, like sand through the hourglass, will continue to flow, and this continuous flowing is the foundation of life—the very rock of the ages.

Wheresoever she was, there was Eden.
—Mark Twain

And wherever you walked, she walked with you.
And wherever you sat, she sat with you.
And whenever you slept, she slept with you.
And whenever you awoke, she awoke with you.
And however you felt, she felt that way too.
And whatever you decided, you decided with her in mind.
And whoever you are now, you are that thanks in part to her.
And this where, when, how, what and who is called the mystery of love.

You can outdistance that which is running after you,
but not what is running inside you.
—*Rwandan proverb*

You may rearrange the furniture in your living room and repaint the walls in your bedroom, but if you have a restless hamster running around a wheel inside you, simply to modify your surroundings will not suffice. The hamster may be temporarily exercised, but he will begin again his mad racing; and as surely as his wheel will come full circle so your anxious dissatisfaction will come around again.

Outward changes may be necessary and even advantageous, but they rarely affect the inward transformation that we so desperately need and want. The thing to do is to ferret out and exterminate that unsettled creature inside.

Opportunities multiply as they are seized.
—Sun-tzu

Sometimes, the break we've been looking for lies at our very feet, and we fail to notice it. Certainly, opportunities abound, but oppressed as we are by the hustle and bustle of modern life, we either miss them completely or simply don't recognize them. When we ease up, take a deep breath, relax, and look around, then we begin to be aware of eventful situations that we may otherwise miss. This awareness is all the preparation opportunity needs. Once we find that one apple at our feet, then we need only look up to discover there's an entire tree's worth, all of them ripe for the picking.

DAY 302 ◆ Unmasking

A man who can fool chiefs, and even gods, must still
face the monsters he himself created.
—old Maori saying

We can play the role of the upwardly mobile, outwardly secure man on the move, but when we settle down alone at night after our frenetic on-the-go day, the truth will out.

Despite what we try to convince others that we are, and even despite what we try to convince ourselves, the truth will out.

We can read a book, watch television, play on the computer, take a pill, or have a drink, yet the truth will out.

The layers upon layers of facade we so dutifully built will only fool those on the outside of the building, and the truth will out.

Time is precious and brief, so let's quit this silly masquerade and face ourselves naked, like on the day we were born.

Nature has made up her mind that what cannot
defend itself shall not be defended.
—*Ralph Waldo Emerson*

Besides its mother, a pup's defense is its irresistible cuteness and cuddliness. What is our defense? Is it our thoughts? It seems to me that our thoughts do more attacking than defending.

Religious and political thought has created every single war.

So what is our defense? Is it not our spirit? The indefatigable human spirit moves us to live and love and procreate, to stand and be counted, to be compassionate and heroic, even under the most trying of circumstances.

Yes, our spirit, the fortification, the very bulwark nature provided each and every one of us, and it is up to each and every one of us to defend his or hers or perish.

Whenever evil befalls us, we ought to ask ourselves, after the first
suffering, how we can turn it into good. So shall
we take occasion, from one bitter root,
to raise perhaps many flowers.
—*Leigh Hunt*

Did you know that below the pain and suffering you may now be feeling lies a sacred seed, an eternal embryo waiting for the smallest cleft, the minutest breach in the concrete of pain for it to bloom, to sprout forth, wild-eyed and fragrant into the sweet air of renewal?

Patience . . .

Patience and faith . . .

Patience and faith . . . and the diminutive acorn becomes the mighty oak.

*One looks back with appreciation to the brilliant teachers, but
with gratitude to those who touched our human feelings.
The curriculum is so much necessary new material, but the
warmth is the vital element for the growing
plant and for the soul of the child.*
—Carl Jung

Just as we are ever aware of the sun that warms and sustains us, so are we aware of those that touched and moved us. Their benevolence resides within us and travels with us when we go out and meet the world.

Without their solicitude we couldn't be what we are today. Without the essential human connections we established with those warmhearted souls, our life would indeed be a bitter and cold affair.

Yes, we learned our multiplication tables and how to read and write, and for that we are appreciative, yet what's this compared with the lessons of love and tenderness we received? Surely our eternal gratitude belongs to those compassionate spirits who ennobled our humanity. Perhaps we can one day repay their kindness by providing in our turn that vital warmth of true human feeling to an uncertain child.

Beauty as we feel it is something indescribable;
what it is or what it means can never be said.
—George Santayana

The butterfly is beauty changing places.
The cat is grace moving across the landscape.
The horse is energy harnessed.
The snake is subtlety playing on the ground.
The sheep are brotherhood on alert.
The geese are the many moving as one.
The goats are self-reliance in action.
The dogs are companionship incarnate.
The ants are organization complete.
The man in the chair is awareness, and
The butterfly is beauty changing places.

No man is rich enough to buy back his past.
—Oscar Wilde

Money, money, money everywhere, and not a dime to spare to pay back the debt of a harsh word, a thoughtless action, or any regrettable deed.

Many arrive at the top but few get there unaccompanied by despair, and it's kind of sad and kind of funny to watch the rich try and stitch an old wound with money, to remold a past that is firmly cast in their head.

Lest you forget it and live to regret it, keep this in mind. No matter what the cost, a thought can't be sold or bought.

*Of course there is no formula for success
except perhaps an unconditional acceptance
of life and what it brings.*
—Arthur Rubinstein

If you could, would you play the game over again, and would you play it the exact same way?

All the bad moves you made, would you make them again and forgive yourself them again?

All the good moves you made, would you make them again and celebrate them again?

Would you again leave your king vulnerable to attack?

Would you again grieve at the loss of your queen and yet be happy that you at least involved her in the game?

Would you again laugh and weep at the fate of your pawns, and praise the subtle movement of your rooks? Would you again send your awkward knights out on uncertain expeditions, and, at times, would you still play your solemn bishops?

Would you play the game over again, the only way you know how, and to the best of your natural ability, and in the exact same way?

DAY 309 ✦ Life Cycle

Whenever a thing changes and alters its nature,
at that moment comes the death of what it was before.
—Lucretius

The infant begins where the newborn ends, and the infant ends where the toddler begins.

The child begins where the toddler ends, and the child ends where the adolescent begins.

The adult begins where the adolescent ends, and the adult ends where middle age begins.

Old age begins where middle age ends, and old age ends where something else altogether unknown begins.

A baby is God's opinion that the world should go on.
—*Carl Sandburg*

From the "Tao of child-rearing" I pass on the following considerations concerning child care:

When he hungers, give him food.
When he thirsts, provide him refreshment.
When he tires, let him lay his head.
When he cries, console him.
When he laughs, laugh with him.
And gently, never forcibly
Guide him through the days.

*No man is an island entire of itself; every man is a piece of the
continent, a part of the main . . . any man's death
diminishes me, because I am involved in mankind; and therefore never
send to know for whom the bell tolls; it tolls for thee.*
—John Donne

A shrug and a sigh and an "I feel sorry for that person" do nothing
to enhance our character as compassionate human beings. In effect, what we're really saying is "I'm superior to that person," and
from our pious pedestal, we look down on that person and from
these holier-than-thou heights to pronounce our judgment.

More to the point, what good has our feeling sorry for people
ever done for them? Has it alleviated their suffering in any way?
Has it assuaged their grief? Will it cure their ills or feed their
stomachs? Surely even the most superficial concern for humanity
exacts more than this flippant "I feel sorry for so-and-so." Better
by far to quietly shed a single tear.

Folly, thou conquerest, and I must yield!
Against stupidity the very gods themselves contend in vain.
—*Friedrich von Schiller*

Stupidity indeed seems to have its own momentum, and once it gets rolling it's hard to stop. Perhaps you can sympathize? No? Well, I'm not buying it. A dullness of mind creeps over all of us at certain times. Try as we might to prevent it, we've all found, to our utter astonishment, the dunce cap sitting atop our heads. The key is to recognize when we are being overcome with foolishness, and extricate ourselves as prudently and as quickly as possible. Otherwise, before we know it, like some never-ending pratfall, stupidity infects our every action, and we stumble from one folly into another.

Every so often, check and make sure it is the thinking cap that you are wearing.

And what is good, Phaedrus, and what is not good,
need we ask anyone to tell us these things?
—*Plato*

Need we ask? And who is it that shall tell us? And why should we accept their answer? Have they spent a day in our shoes? Surely, past a certain age what is "good" for us is ours to embrace and not another's to shackle us with. Keep faith with your own innate goodness. Listen . . . listen closely for that "still small voice" that is your portion of the divine. It will guide and comfort, serve and preserve you. When you question, it will answer, and its answers hold within them all the morality you'll ever need.

No matter how far you have gone on a wrong road, turn back.
—Turkish proverb

Better late than never, and better now than forever . . .

So you got involved in a bogus cause, or found yourself in disbelief about what you believed for so many years, or finally discovered you're in the wrong occupation. None of this is uncommon.

What's uncommon is having the courage to turn back. What's uncommon is being willing and able to change, no matter how late in the game.

To admit to yourself and to others that you were mistaken requires unusual strength of character, but it requires this and more to fix your mistake. Such is the stuff from which heroes are made.

*I have discovered that all human evil comes from this, man's being
unable to sit still and quiet in a room alone.*
—*Blaise Pascal*

Think of all the mess and mayhem caused by those of us with restless spirits. Not being able to spend untroubled moments with ourselves, we go out and trouble others. If discomfort and uneasiness live with us in our own homes, even when alone, then how can we expect to relate in a peaceful and communal way with others? We can't. If we are inwardly conflicted, then it will show outwardly. This is an observable fact. Therefore, it would seem to be of the utmost importance for us to do the work—and do it now—necessary to living at peace within ourselves.

Loneliness and Solitude

Language has created the word loneliness to express the pain
of being alone, and the word solitude
to express the glory of being alone.
—Paul Tillich

As vast as the distance between the moon and the sun is the distance between loneliness and solitude.

Solitude refreshes and awakens while loneliness degrades and debases. Solitude is creative while loneliness is tedious. Solitude promotes peace of mind while loneliness engenders restlessness. Those knowing the salutary effects of solitude deliberately seek out times alone to be quietly contemplative, while those who don't know this desperately seek to avoid such times. This profound distinction between solitude and loneliness requires our deepest attention, as it may be the distinction that makes all the difference.

Therefore do not be anxious about tomorrow,
for tomorrow will be anxious for itself.
Let the day's own trouble be sufficient
for the day.
—Matthew 6:34

A perfectly sensible saying such as this one flows so easily from the mouths of prophets, and even to us ordinary folks the meaning stated here seems self-evident. Nonetheless, which one of us doesn't on occasion get anxious about tomorrow?

Though we can clearly see based on experience that each day has its sufficient share of burdens, we yet insist on adding tomorrow's uncertainty to the platter. It almost seems as if we're afraid to commit fully to today, so we bring in the specter of tomorrow to excuse ourselves for being noncommittal about the present.

And what does all this psychological forecasting do for us? Well, for starters, it makes us insecure, provides us with an uncomfortable undercurrent of fear, in addition to diminishing the fullness of today. Consequently, we may want to consider abandoning this unwholesome practice before we harass all our todays with thoughts of tomorrow.

Not everything that can be counted counts,
and not everything that counts can be counted.
—*Albert Einstein*

A miser counting his pennies thinks a child counting the stars is foolish. But the child knows what the miser doesn't, and that is that every star counts for something while every penny amounts to virtually nothing. Let us take a detailed account of our lives and see if what we enumerate as important is really worthy of that designation. Perhaps we are tallying incorrectly, simply engaging in a dead reckoning that needlessly leaves us unfulfilled and anxious. Balance, that's what's needed, a proper balance between our practical and spiritual accounts.

I believe that a scientist looking at nonscientific problems
is just as dumb as the next guy.
—*Richard Feynman*

As Plato convincingly showed through Socrates, simply because a man is an expert in one field, doesn't mean he's an expert in the all-important field of living. Van Gogh, an expert painter, was tormented. Beethoven, an expert musician, was tormented. Nietzsche, an expert philosopher, was tormented. We all seem to be in the same leaky ark when it comes to the problems of living.

Love, truth, beauty, compassion, fear, anger, hatred, and sorrow, from the floor sweeper to the president, from the nuclear physicist to the gardener, these problematic concepts belong to each and every soul, and each and every soul is equally qualified to discover their meaning. A doctorate degree in love and in truth, or in sorrow and in anger, does not exist save for the one you complete through living.

The Tao that can be told of is not the eternal Tao.
The Way that can be followed is not the eternal Way.
—Lao-tzu

Accept and you shall be told. Follow and you shall be led. What you are told may be false. Where you are led may be to misery. Stop and think for yourself and you shall discover, and what you shall discover will be uniquely yours, because it was discovered and molded by and within you.

Henceforth, wherever you may go, your discovery will go with you. Henceforth, whatever you may be told, you will listen to with the self-assurance born of insight. After all, eternity is a word that stands for a concept that means nothing but what we ourselves understand it to mean.

Fantasy, abandoned by reason, produces impossible monsters;
united with it, she is the mother of the arts
and the origin of marvels.
—Francisco José de Goya

Our ability to imagine is what makes human beings unique among the earth's creatures. Other animals besides us have the capacity to reason, think, and communicate, but only man has the capacity to imagine.

Imagination creates gods and devils, heavens and hells. From this hallowed ground springs the grandeur of art, and the amazing discoveries of science. From this unholy ground springs the madness of man, and his diabolical inventions.

As the imagination is a sword that can cut both ways, we must be careful to carry the shield of reason when we employ it. Imagination detached from reason becomes the scourge of the world. To illustrate this point, let me remind you of the words of the *Bhagavad Gita* remembered and spoken by J. Robert Oppenheimer, the head of the Manhattan Project, upon seeing the first atomic bomb test explosion: "I am become Death, the destroyer of worlds."

No bird soars too high if he soars with his own wings.
—William Blake

Self-reliance creates its own foundation on which to build. Constantly reshaping and refining, the self-reliant person constructs his own life from the materials at hand. In doing so, he understands both his abilities and limitations and works with the former and tries to go beyond the latter. He is not easily dissuaded from his purpose, for he is purposeful of mind. Yet he doesn't reach beyond his grasp, nor does he rush toward what lies ahead. Patience, he knows, will yet enable him to place the steeple atop his cathedral.

Now I see the secret of the making of the best persons.
It is to grow in the open air and to eat and sleep with the earth.
—Walt Whitman

Walt Whitman didn't live in a tent on the prairie, but he was grounded. So grounded that he soared. And that is entirely the point. The best people are grounded, have a sense of origins, and breathe naturally. The best people are at home in every season and happily take their meals in the sun or rain, and laugh heartily and cry heartily and live and love and falter, knowing that "every atom belonging to me as good belongs to you." The best people invite this secret into their souls.

*Adversity has the effect of eliciting talents, which in prosperous
circumstances would have lain dormant.*
—Horace

Otherwise unfamiliar to us, our better self emerges betimes
through hardship and misery. Unimaginable circumstances lead to
imaginative responses, because misfortune provokes complete action. Given the opportunity, we who think ourselves cowardly
may yet act heroically, and awaken hitherto fallow abilities. The
time will come in our lives when all of us will be required to
either take action and live happily, or succumb to the weight of
events and die miserably, though we may yet still breathe.

✦ Holding a Tune

Oh, give us the man who sings at his work.
—*Thomas Carlyle*

If your work is such that it makes you feel at times like singing, then you are lucky indeed. Alas, we can't all be members of the Staples Singers, or star in a Puccini opera. Sadly, most of us walk about the hallways of our offices in various states of muted distress. Maybe though, if we begin to hum a little tune, the atmosphere will change and the scenery will brighten.

Now, I'm not suggesting that you suddenly start singing a capella at work, as this could easily be misconstrued as your having lost your marbles; however, maintaining a sweet inward melody may serve to alleviate some of the stress, may serve to lighten the load.

A good rest is half the work.
—Yugoslav proverb

In this fast-paced, computerized world many of us consider taking time out for a good rest as irresponsible as falling asleep on sentry duty (take a deep breath). Somehow, busyness has now become synonymous with progress, and we feel that we're cheating ourselves if our new sacred cow, busyness, is not constantly chewing the cud (take another deep breath).

But what better preparation for the travail of modern life than the recentering and harnessing of energy that a good rest affords? Without proper relaxation, we become nervous and irritable, and have trouble focusing, thereby generating even more work, and so the cycle of frantic activity continues (and another deep breath). Meanwhile, within the stillness and quietude of a good rest breeds the necessary energy to be completely engaged in the work at hand (and another deep breath).

Furthermore, proper rest alleviates stress, and less stress means better mental and physical health, and better mental and physical health means . . . means a lot! (First one more deep breath.)

*The important thing is not to stop questioning. Curiosity has its own
reason for existing. One cannot help but be in awe when he
contemplates the mysteries of eternity, of life, of the
marvelous structure of reality. It is enough if one tries merely
to comprehend a little of this mystery every day.
Never lose a holy curiosity.*
—Albert Einstein

We may wonder about the mystery, but the mystery wonders not
about us. If we ask not, it won't answer; if we inquire not, it won't
reveal; if we have not passion, it will seem passionless; if we are
indifferent, it will be indifferent to us.

Start today the never-ending inquiry into the startling mystery
that is being alive. After all, if we consider for only a moment
the incredible commingling of events that conspired to put us
here, then this alone should inspire enough wonderment to get
us started.

The choice between living a life in the full bosom of awe, or
living a hollow unexamined life devoid of the sanctity of mystery,
resides within each of our breasts.

DAY 328 ✦ Returning Home

God is at home,
it's we who have gone out for a walk.
—Meister Eckehart

If we know the way, returning home is simple. Recognizing that we have strayed from the spirit's true dwelling place, and having the courage to return there, this is difficult—for awakening is always difficult. Mostly, we prefer to remain slumbering in the status quo. We are comfortable with its routine and pleased with its familiarity. Nothing troubles and disturbs us more than a blow to our habits, because we are indistinguishable from them—we have become monotony and routine.

Cease today the spinning of your wheels and meditate upon that holiness that lives within you. For long enough have we wandered aimlessly. It's time to head home now. It's time now to sit by the hearth, to feel the warmth of the eternal firelight. God awaits us.

I enjoyed my own nature to the fullest, and we all know that there lies happiness, although, to soothe one another mutually, we occasionally pretend to condemn such joys as selfishness.
—*Albert Camus*

If you had to be locked for seventy-odd years in a room with somebody, with whom would you choose to be locked? I hope to God that you said yourself. Otherwise, the days ahead will indeed weigh heavily on your shoulders.

To choose you, is that selfish? Is "me first" in the profoundest sense really being selfish?

What good is a mother who puts her child first and falls apart in the process?

Isn't the best captain the one who has a healthy regard for his own well-being?

I submit to you that if you follow selfishness to its logical end, you will find there complete selflessness.

DAY 330 ✦ Something Lost
Is Something Gained

*When the heart grieves over what is lost,
the spirit rejoices over what is left.*
—Sufi saying

In the strange way of the world, it is better to grieve than have nothing to grieve for. What could be said for the quality of our love, if, when it's gone, we shed not a tear? Surely the depth of our sorrow should be equal to the depth of our love. What is life but a series of comings and goings? Therefore, let us unashamedly mourn our losses, all the while being careful not to slip into the quagmire of self-pity, remembering that even as the apple tree looks decrepit and barren in the fall, so it again will blossom and be fragrant come spring.

Truth sits upon the lips of dying men.
—*Matthew Arnold*

The urge to confess, to acknowledge what we've so carefully kept hidden, is a powerful one. The sick and infirm, those on the threshold of death, usually feel compelled to say their piece before they die. Something within strongly suggests to them that they own up to the truth that was their life, and so we have the deathbed confession. But why wait until the end to unburden our hearts? Why wait until the end to speak lovingly to those that we love? Better to speak now. Better to clear our conscience today rather than tomorrow, when it may be too late.

It is easier to stay out than get out.
—Mark Twain

How many times have we, like a fly in a web, got wrapped into something we then have a terrible time extricating ourselves from? Too many. This is because we don't think before we leap. We too easily get involved in a job or a project of some kind or another and find ourselves trapped in the gravity of unintended circumstances.

Once caught in these Kafkaesque situations, we find that the way out is not so clearly defined. Others are now relying on us and we don't want to let them down, we need the money, we have our own expectations to answer to, and many and more excuses find us stuck in intolerable positions. Far less distressful, is it not, not to get involved in the first place than to get uninvolved once we're involved. Just say no!

The young have aspirations that never come to pass,
the old have reminiscences of what never happened.
—*Saki*

Dreams of what may be and reflections on what could have been. All of us engage in this sort of mental gymnastics. We flip forward and we roll backward. Somewhere in all this tumbling lies the inescapable present. Though you are young and have lofty aspirations, you are having them in the present; and though you are old and have regrettable reminiscences, you too are having them in the present.

Hopefully, while you're dreaming of making it big or ruing missed opportunities, your house doesn't catch on fire. On the other hand, if it did, surely that would awaken you from your reveries; surely then you'd know what the present means and leap into action.

We never know the worth of water
till the well is dry.
—English proverb

Take your friends or family, husband or wife, child or lover, bank account or yourself for granted at your own risk. There should be a sign posted at crosswalks that says Warning, Person Who Takes Life for Granted May Be Crossing.

Not much is more nauseating than those privileged who do not recognize and appreciate their privileges. Of course, they too have a right to be unhappy, indeed they usually are, but it's the cavalier attitude to all they have that shames them.

Did the sun yet again leave great swaths of colored beams in the clouds as it set? Then rejoice.

Did you by chance see a bluebird in the blue sky? Then rejoice.

Did you happen by a lily in the valley? Then rejoice.

Do you have food and clothes aplenty? Then rejoice.

Are you of sound mind and body? Then rejoice.

Do you know that life is ephemeral? Then rejoice.

When the stars threw down their spears
And water'd heaven with their tears
Did he smile his work to see?
Did he who made the lamb make thee?
—*William Blake*

Have you taken a moment to consider the kangaroo? Here we have a grazing creature not unlike a deer or sheep, save that instead of four hooves with which to gambol about, it stands somewhat upright and has two large hooves and a thick tail with which to—of all things—hop about. How marvelously ungainly!

What about the bat? Have you at all considered it? This creature, with teeny little hands and a cape and not a single discernible feather, is completely blind, and yet its primary mode of transportation is to fly. How strangely moving!

Or the caterpillar? A slothful down-bedecked worm that one day decides to intern itself in its own silk sarcophagus, only to emerge sometime hence as a busy, beautiful butterfly. How mysteriously miraculous!

What about man's best friend, a dog, a possessor of such wit and cunning that it somehow manages to be sleeping on our couches, have you at all considered this beast? How audaciously ingenious it is!

Really now, a platypus? We won't even begin to discuss this confused creature. Did he indeed smile his work to see?

Do we?

Happiness is as a butterfly which, when pursued, is always
beyond our grasp, but which if you will sit down quietly,
may alight upon you.
—*Nathaniel Hawthorne*

The pursuit of happiness is a lovely phrase but a frustrating endeavor. Happiness can no more be pursued than the phoenix. As we reflect on the occasions when we were most happy, we will see that happiness is a by-product, a feeling that comes over us while we are otherwise engaged. It's only later that we realize we were truly happy on a particular occasion. Not a goal to be achieved but a result of achievement, happiness is a personal vision as unique to each of us as our features. Still your soul and the bird of happiness may yet alight on your shoulder.

Tell me and I'll forget; show me and I may remember;
involve me and I'll understand.
—Chinese proverb

Tell me how to type and I'm likely to grow quickly weary of your explanation. Show me how to type and I may better grasp your explanation. But let me put my fingers to the keys, and soon I'll be composing a letter. Furthermore, once I have understood how to type by doing—rather than just having memorized typing procedure—this ability to type will remain with me, and not fade like a memory. Memories fade because they are images, and images begin to dull with time. Whereas understanding implies an internal assimilation that resists the deterioration of time.

*The world is so empty if one thinks only of mountains, rivers and
cities; but to know someone here and there who thinks
and feels with us, and though distant, is close to us
in spirit—this makes the earth for us an inhabited garden.*
—*Johann Wolfgang von Goethe*

Without those bosom buddies we know and love as kindred spirits, life indeed seems barren. But to take a walk near to heaven in the lovely mountains, knowing we have a friend in the city, to sit quietly by a green flowing river, knowing we have a friend in town, enhances the very nature of our experiences.

To know that we have someone akin enough to our hearts that we may openly share with that person the stories of our journey, and he or she will openly listen and understand without being harshly critical or piously judgmental, this is as much of Eden as we're likely to find. Therefore, gather ye the rosebuds of friendship while ye may.

*The myriad creatures carry on their backs the yin and embrace
in their arms the yang, and are the blending of the
generative forces of the two.*
—*Lao-tzu*

Lao-tzu was the keeper of the gate and the undisputed king of understanding the duality of life. Duality: Duo. Double. Dialogue. Dichotomy. Dice. Duel: It takes two to tango. Matter and Spirit. Body and Soul. Good and Evil. Positive and Negative. Black and White. Happy and Sad. Beautiful and Ugly. Life and Death. Yin and Yang. Male and Female. As the song says, "you can't have one without the other."

The supple merging between day and night is a time of stillness and quiet; the supple merging between night and day is a time of awakening and activity, and together these make up the twilight of our lives.

DAY 340 ✦ Visibility

To us also, through every star, through every blade of grass, is not God made visible if we will open our minds and our eyes.
—Thomas Carlyle

Yes, we all may partake of the divine feast. It's not an exclusive club. The God market has not been cornered by the gurus, priests, rabbis, and such, but is there for all with eyes to see, or with ears to hear, or with the heart to feel.

God is in those visions of sugar plums dancing in your head, and in the tree trunk as well as the cat's meow.

No need to look to others for spiritual guidance, simply look.

No need to listen to religious preaching, simply listen.

No need to take honey to the beehive.

It's all about and in us, this spirit that pervades all. Find it where you may.

It is a man's own mind, not his enemy or foe,
that lures him to evil ways.
—*Buddha*

Allow not enmity to take hold in your mind, as it will engender your own imbalance.

Allow not animus to take hold in your mind, as it will do you ill.

Allow not animosity to take hold in your mind, unless you desire spite for your daily bread.

Allow not rancor to ruffle your feathers, lest you find your own mind disheveled.

Harbor not antipathies, for this in itself is repugnant.

Engage not in antagonism, for this readily leads to regrettable action.

Finally, follow not the way of hostility, for this leads unto the loss of freedom.

Men's natures are alike;
it is their habits that carry them apart.
—Confucius

Constantly redefining ourselves, changeable from one day to the next, from one moment to the next, we are mental chameleons. To our friends and family, we may stay roughly the same color, but we know better, we know how truly mutable we are. One train of thought finds us sanguine, and another finds us blue, and all within two minutes. From within this inner prism we go out and meet life, and though we may seem colorless to others, we know full well that we encompass the entire spectrum—and that they do as well.

Wear as often you will the color you think is yours—or the one you have been summarily painted with—but none of us is fooled. Most of us can see the rainbow despite the cast of the sky.

What I am is good enough
if I would only be it openly.
—*Carl Rogers*

If you're a crank, then be a crank until you're finished with cranki-ness. If you're a cynic, at least be a profound one, like Diogenes. Maybe you're insecure and uncertain. That's okay. Stay with those feelings until you've had your fill, and then you may go beyond them. Deal completely with what you are; know all your foibles, idiosyncrasies, troubles, and insecurities. Take them to heart, and not your wish to be something else. That something else doesn't actually exist; it remains an idea, a false ideal. What exists is the unique you, with all its complications. This is what needs to be refined and cultivated. In a word, be yourself. Only in this way will you overcome what needs to be overcome.

DAY 344 ✦ Religious Spirit

Be still, and know that I am God.
—Psalm 46:10

I've heard tell about a person who, after abusing alcohol and drugs, found religion, and then abused that as well. He traded one addiction for another.

His so-called conversion compelled him to try to convert everyone else: He would tell all and sundry to watch the 700 *Club;* he would hand out religious brochures, press phone numbers into people's hands, insist that they go to his church meetings, and altogether so hound and harass people about his God that he ended up losing his family and his business. Strangely, he acted as if everyone that crossed his path had never before heard of the Divine.

The knowledge of the fabric of God is uniquely woven into us all, and it is for each of us in his or her own way to stitch the quilt of religion—and this quilt is a lifetime in the making. An evangelical television show, a religious flier, or another person, no matter how eager, cannot do it for us. Indeed, such an aggressive proselytizer strikes most of us as disingenuous, and usually succeeds only in annoying and alienating those of us who are earnestly searching for that which is God within.

Let's let our actions, rather than our rhetoric, speak for our religiousness.

PITY, n. A failing sense of exemption, inspired by contrast.
—Ambrose Bierce

All of us stranded at the traffic light stared with pity at the homeless man who dropped his worldly belongings on the ground in his struggle to retrieve his shoe that had gotten stuck in the mud.

Is not pity a self-serving and superior attitude to take? Presumably this man has as many happy moments as we do, albeit of a different kind than ours. A warm meal, I'm certain this makes him happy. A safe, dry, and comfortable place to lay his head, I'm certain this too makes him happy. On the other hand, these things don't make us happy, at least not anymore—and perhaps they never have. Granted, a gourmet meal in a fancy restaurant may still make us momentarily happy, or a brand-new king-size bed with a down comforter and feather pillows may yet make us momentarily happy, but, as I said, this is of a different kind.

If we must engage in pity, let's at least leave it at home in the mirror where it belongs, and bring compassion with us on the road.

To be interested in the changing seasons is a happier state of mind
than to be hopelessly in love with spring.
—*George Santayana*

Yes, that's it, is it not? To be interested. To be truly interested in life's changing fortunes. To be interested in the best of times and the worst of times. After all, to be interested also implies a willingness to learn, does it not? And learning means active participation; and active participation means living.

Thus, enkindle within the flame of interest, and you will burn brightly through all the vicissitudes of a lifetime. Do not worry and long so for the spring. It knows what it's doing. Winter will walk away soon enough. All things in their own due time.

Many changes a climate make, and many moments, a life.

DAY 347 ✦ Technology

Men have become the tools of their tools.
—Henry David Thoreau

Our brains simply couldn't handle the massive influx of available information—information accumulated over centuries of learning and discovery—and so we made a tool to help us store and sort all this information. That tool is the computer, a device akin to human memory that the mind invented, a device that prevents us from crashing our own hard drives. This is an amazing tool, an incredible invention, and one whose possibilities are just beginning to come into focus. However, we must keep in mind, despite its appeal, that it is still just a tool, and should be treated accordingly. Don't become enslaved to it. Don't let it monopolize your free time. Don't allow it to become your main means of communication with others. Remember, there's no substitute for human interaction; there's no substitute for feeling the soft hand of another on your shoulder. Besides, virtual sunshine isn't going to cut it.

DAY 348 ✦ Adaptation

*It is not the strongest of the species that survive, nor the
most intelligent, but the one most responsive to change.*
—*Charles Darwin*

Technology is evolving at breakneck speed, and we are hard-
pressed to keep pace. How we, as individuals, respond psychologically to these rapid changes makes all the difference to the quality
of our lives. If we resist change, if we struggle against it, we will
soon feel overwhelmed and alienated. Such feelings breed anxiety
and despair. Conversely, if we are open and adaptable to the
continuous evolution that is the modern age we will feel energized
and invigorated by change. Such feelings of enthusiasm for the
new allow us not merely to survive, but to thrive. Our well-being
is directly linked to our adaptability.

Money may be the husk of many things, but not the kernel.
It buys you food, but not appetite; medicine, but not health;
acquaintances, but not friends; servants, but not loyalty;
days of joy; but not peace or happiness.
—*Henrik Ibsen*

Throughout the ages, those with and those without money have described ad nauseam how money does nothing to solve the intrinsic problem of living a happy life; indeed, most describe it as the greatest hindrance to such a life, and yet the admonishments about the evil allure of money are the most consistently ignored admonishments of all. Most people will believe it when they hear that vanity, jealousy, envy, and spite are harmful, but when it comes to saying money is harmful, all that you might say falls on selectively deaf ears. Amazing how swiftly people become disengaged when you try to mention the possible negative consequences of pursuing money. They look at you as if for some incomprehensible reason you started speaking Swahili. At any rate, the "notes" on money and its capacity for engendering enlightenment are clear and consistent. So . . . enough said.

You may delay, but time will not.
—Benjamin Franklin

Take your time, "why do today what you can do the day after tomorrow?" and before you know it twenty-five years, an entire generation, has slipped by. (Tick) Before you know it, you're looking back in longing. (Tock) Time is relentless; therefore, relent to it. (Tick) Why follow the hands as they move in circles around the clock? (Tock) Why belabor the minutes with your attention to them? (Tick) Get on with it. (Tock) Be about your business. (Tick) This is not to say rush headlong through life, for, as the proverb states truly, "With time and patience the mulberry leaf becomes a silk gown." (Tock) But at least be somewhat in earnest so that before you know it you'll look back not in longing but in wonder, wonder at the timeless quality of your life. (Tick-Tock, Tick-Tock)

✦ The Journey of Life

A good traveler has no fixed plans,
and is not intent on arriving.
—Lao-tzu

The journey is the destination and life is the journey. Without a fixed plan, we intuitively adapt to this wondrous journey called living. A wayfarer and not a tourist, we discover uncharted byways and experience the native territory of this vast country road we call life. Whereas if we're only intent on arriving we steer a narrow course, missing much, owing to our myopic focusing on a set destination. A good traveler adapts and leaves room for spontaneity and does not live and die by an itinerary.

DAY 352 ✦ Love Makes the World Go Round

*Let us live and love, my Lesbia, and value at a penny all the talk of
crabbed old men. Suns may set and rise again: for us, when our
brief light has set, there's the sleep of perpetual night.*
Give me a thousand kisses.
—*Catullus*

I never tire of writing about love because love never tires of being
written about.

Ever refreshing, ever in bloom, love, as the poets say, makes
the world go round.

Not simply an emotion, nor a feeling, nor a state of mind,
but an entire spiritual essence, this is love.

Love is as alive as the soil and the flowers, and is as bright
and immediate as the sunshine.

Love is as vast and various as the universal stars that pattern
eternity, and is as unquenchable as the oceans. Love is not yours,
nor mine, nor hers, nor his, but simply is.

The old law about "an eye for an eye" leaves everybody blind.
—Martin Luther King, Jr.

The endless agony of revenge: I've been wronged so I will wrong you, and you in your turn will wrong another, and he or she another, and so on until all of us are blind with hatred, bloodthirsty with anger, and desperate to lash out. Terribly sad but real, this ugly pattern, this self-perpetuating madness.

We see it in our cities and from our governments and now most everybody has an ax to grind, and they are looking for a head to grind it on. We've lost all proportion and it's become an eye for two eyes and an ear.

Forgive, and you shall feel the oppressive weight of enmity fall from your spirit.

Harbor vengeful thoughts and you shall live in strife.

It's really quite simple: Without the capacity to forgive, a person has no chance of being at peace.

One may not reach the dawn save by the path of the night.
—*Kahlil Gibran*

Sorrow is familiar to all of us. It is one of the ingredients common to all humanity, like love and death. What is uncommon, however, are those who have ended sorrow within. I have yet to meet such a person, though I have read of many. Even so, these singular individuals have existed. They traveled the rugged road of suffering to get to the path of light; they stared down life's demons and emerged radiant.

Consider this: What one can do in the realm of the spirit, another can do. The dawn lingers just over the horizon, it is mad with beauty, full to the brim with dancing rainbows, and we need only carve our way through the mountainous black night to see it.

Into each life some rain must fall,
some days be dark and dreary.
—Henry Wadsworth Longfellow

One moment, we may be found enjoying a temperate afternoon on our own personal blueberry hill; and the next, we may find ourselves swept headlong into the swift current of troubling events like a toy tugboat in the rapids.

Strange and dramatic how quickly and unexpectedly we can get caught up in the disturbing flow of negative circumstances. From here to there, from bliss to despair, in seemingly mere moments. Equally strange and no less dramatic are those times when we are suddenly and mysteriously plucked from the raging river of oppressive events and find ourselves again relaxing on our blueberry hill. From there to here, from despair to bliss, in seemingly mere moments.

Yes, it would appear that the pendulum does swing both ways, and that for every dusk, a dawn; for every low, a high tide, and it is with this understanding that we can weather even the most furious storm.

We are here to add what we can to life,
not to get what we can from it.
—William Osler

Our upbringing promotes getting rather than giving. We journey through this life with an eye toward acquiring instead of creating, and this does us, as well as our fellow man, a great disservice. Acquisitiveness breeds waste, strife, dissatisfaction, and selfishness. Mostly, we remain unaware of this consuming habit of mind because we have been so steeped in this culture of procurement that we have become inured to it.

Perhaps a reexamination, a new approach, is in order. A state of mind that tends toward creative contribution as opposed to covetousness travels an entirely different path. Such a mind adds richness and variety to itself.

*God expects but one thing of you, and that is that you should
come out of yourself insofar as you are a created being made
and let God be God in you.*
—Meister Eckehart

The cork remains tightly sealed in the top of the bottle, yet the heady aroma and bittersweet flavor, the very richness and abundance of the Spirit within, await unsullied its liberation.

And so it is that what we don't feel now in no way diminishes the fullness within us, the plenitude that once upon a time was manifest.

Perhaps all we require is the proper tool, the as-yet-undiscovered utensil that will release the stopper, and allow the free flow of the nectar that by rights is ours.

Our obligation, then, our urgent responsibility, continues to be to discover that elusive tool; or, better still, for each of us to be the artisan of our own instrument of freedom.

Everything else seems to be so sadly beside the point. Everything else seems to be but another cork in the bottle.

Facts don't cease to exist because they are ignored.
—*Aldous Huxley*

The fact is I'm tired. I can ignore this fact and maybe inadvertently step off the curb in front of an oncoming bus, or I can deal with the fact of my fatigue and get some rest. In other words, by ignoring one fact we may find ourselves facing a more complex set of facts that we can't so easily slough off.

Ignoring or escaping from what *is* may be convenient in the short term, but in the long run, it is disadvantageous. Denials accumulate to become burdens we openly wear on our shoulders.

It's much healthier to deal with the facts of life, no matter how inconvenient, as they arise. In this way we retain a kind of buoyancy that enables us to better handle any troubling events that should come our way. Not weighted down with unfinished business, we are more capable of dealing with present circumstances.

There are two ways of spreading light:
to be the candle or the mirror that reflects it.
—Edith Wharton

Generosity does not necessarily require a purse. Charity has its place, but it is not the last word in generosity. One may also be generous of spirit. Somehow this seems to be the noblest form of generosity. To possess such an abundance of affection and love that you give of yourself to others in need is truly wondrous. A generous spirit receives—through the reflection of a grateful face—a generosity equal to what was given. A more perfect exchange does not exist. At this point, the giver and receiver become one, and a portion of divinity falls to the earth.

Don't think for a moment that you can't be of such a generous nature. I'm sure a situation of this magnitude has already occurred in your life, and that you were equal to it. Perhaps an occasion for such an exchange will happen again, and this time you will know it is the best part of you that is answering the call.

We must, indeed, all hang together or, most assuredly,
we shall all hang separately.
—*Benjamin Franklin*

It will no longer suffice to hang together only as a family, a neighborhood, or a nation. We need to hang together as citizens of the earth. This has now become essential.

Unfortunately, hanging separately will continue to be the norm until each of us decides to work toward becoming whole, to reject the notion of separateness.

As long as we feel separate, then separation will prevail, along with the conflict between people and nations it engenders. If we can't even cooperate with ourselves, then surely cooperation with our neighbors is highly unlikely.

Self-integration is the first step. We must get ourselves together, make a vase out of the psychological fragments, before we can ever hope to be a vessel of goodwill and cooperation. All the pieces are there; we need only pick them up.

DAY 361 ✦ Self-Help

Voluntary loneliness, isolation from others,
is the readiest safeguard against the unhappiness
that may arise out of human relations.
—Sigmund Freud

It is not uncommon for any of us to feel, at times, lonely and unloved. Feeling that those we spend so much time thinking about and caring for are ungrateful, this too is not unusual. Perhaps the solution to our sense of loneliness lies within us. Maybe if we spent a little more time considering our own well-being rather than constantly thinking of those around us, we might find more fulfillment.

Don't think for a moment that if you do give more concern to yourself that you are being selfish. On the contrary, what better way to make those around you happier than by making yourself happier? So, my suggestion to you is, do some of the things you like to do, but may have had to put off doing, due to your immoderate concern with problems of others. Take the time to engage your spirit by going for a walk, talking with a friend, reading a book, or anything else that may interest you but that you have sacrificed out of a false sense of duty. In this way, you may find that happiness will once again be your friend.

There is only one science, love; only one riches, love; only one policy, love. To make love is all the law, and the prophets.
—*Anatole France*

If I had my way I'd write every day about love,
For what is a today anyway without love . . . ?
You can ignore, abuse, and try to corrupt it
Yet it is always there, even as the sun is always there, day or
    night.

✦ Distinguishing Traits

How much better a thing it is to be envied than to be pitied.
—Herodotus

Each of us has one or more enviable qualities. Maybe it's your eyes or wit, your hands or thoughtfulness, your sense of humor or hair, your intelligence or nose, your creative ability or shoulders, your empathy or lips—to be sure, both inwardly and outwardly, something about you is special. Make room for what is special about you to bear fruit. Cultivate your God-given distinctiveness. Important in your own way, be thrilled that you possess memorable qualities that distinguish you.

Rather than crave what you lack, why not let ripen what you have?

*One day Alice came to a fork in the road and saw a Cheshire cat
in a tree. "Which road do I take?" she asked.
"Where do you want to go?" was his response.
"I don't know," Alice answered.
"Then," said the cat, "it doesn't matter."*
—Lewis Carroll

Just as you must focus the camera in order to take a proper picture, so you must focus your mind to achieve anything of importance. Without focus, it doesn't matter which way we turn. Without an aim, we wander aimlessly.

To fulfill our aspirations, we need to know what we aspire to. Finding and then zeroing in on a purpose is the difficult part. The first order of business should be to hone in on a goal.

Once you commit body and soul to an intention, the way to go becomes less vague. With a clearly defined goal comes the passion needed to see to its fruition.

Having an absorbing mission creates its own energy. This is not to say that things will then come easy, only that they will come.

*Truly the light is sweet, and a pleasant thing it is for
the eyes to behold the sun.*
—*Ecclesiastes* 11:7

Sometimes it takes a great effort of will, a reaching deep down into the reserves of energy, to keep our eyes open wide enough not to fall into the thrall of vice or madness.

Patience, my brothers and sisters, thou art good. Don't allow a few missteps to spoil this truth. Don't let a rebellious head blacken the sanctity of your heart.

Venture forth with the knowledge that your soul will shine despite the darkness, even as a diamond shines amid the coal. Henceforward carry in your breast the knowledge that redemption abides in your every step, and that absolution moves to the rhythm of your breath.

No longer deny the riches you were blessed with; avail yourself of that measure of love and beauty that by rights is yours. Free yourself from guilt and behold life in its abundance; how well it is for you to live happily, profoundly.

Act now as if you belonged here, as if this inexplicable, magical place called earth was created solely for your edification.

Afterword

Believe nothing, no matter where you read it, or who said it,
no matter if I have said it, unless it agrees with
your own reason and your own common sense.
—Buddha

I despise quotations.
—Ralph Waldo Emerson

Finally, in conclusion, let me say just this.
—Peter Sellers

That's all, folks!
—Bugs Bunny

The preceding book has been brought to you
by the letter L and the number 1.
—Sesame Street

About the Author

Writer, editor, and part-time shepherd, Scott M. Gallagher was born in Philadelphia, Pennsylvania, in 1965. After graduating from high school in Moorestown, New Jersey, he drove across the country to live in Southern California. He attended community college and the University of California, Los Angeles, before starting his own business. It was, ironically, during this time that he began to study literature and write. One of his poems was chosen to be featured on ABCNews.com, for National Poetry Month 1998.

Scott Gallagher became editor of The Mind, Body & Soul Network, the Internet's Largest Self-Help Site, on August 1, 1998. Along with writing the "Daily Meditations" column for MBS, he also writes the biweekly newsletter.

On the side, he can be found teaching sheep herding and competing in herding events with his Old English sheepdog, Apollo. Scott Gallagher lives in Southern California with his son, Dylan.

About The Mind, Body & Soul Network

The Mind, Body & Soul Network, the creation of Alchemy Communications, Inc. (www.alchemy.net), was designed to provide Internet users with an abundance of information, products, and services to improve the quality of their lives.

Dedicated to personal growth, physical health, and spiritual awareness, The Mind, Body & Soul Network (www.mindbodysoul.com) and its partner, New Age Cities (www.newagecities.com), continue to provide Internet users with holistic, new-age solutions to age-old problems.